SUCCESSFUL SELLING SOLUTIONS

Test, monitor and constantly
improve your selling skills

Julian Clay

THORO*g*OOD

Published by Thorogood
10-12 Rivington Street
London EC2A 3DU

Telephone: 020 7749 4748
Fax: 020 7729 6110
Email: info@thorogood.ws
Web: www.thorogood.ws

A CIP catalogue record for this book is
available from the British Library.

HB: ISBN 1 85418 298 6
PB: ISBN 1 85418 242 0

Designed and typeset by Driftdesign.

Printed in India by Replika Press Pvt. Ltd.

Special discounts for bulk
quantities of Thorogood books
are available to corporations,
institutions, associations and
other organisations. For more
information contact Thorogood
by telephone on 020 7749 4748,
by fax on 020 7729 6110, or
email us: info@thorogood.ws

Acknowledgements

I would like to thank:

- *Doug Dews*, a former Sales Operations Manager, for the benefit of his experience as well as his advice on negotiation and closing a sale

- *Kathleen Canning*, a Training Solutions Manager, for her help on presentations, proposals and ideas regarding the book's tables and charts

- *Andrew Mills*, a Sales and Marketing Director, for his help on targeting new companies, managing accounts and analysing sales performance

- *Martin Clay*, an experienced Sales Manager, for his advice on questioning techniques and in particular, for his help on the structure and content

- *Lawrie Siteman*, a Group Managing Director, for his contribution on preparation, sales development and introductions to new accounts

- *Mike Brewster*, a Sales Consultant, for advising me on the material used in the example of a proposal and with *Ben Hedger*, for incorporating many of the sales models as part of their daily routine since 2000.

- *The SPIN® strategy* – Huthwaite Research Group

- *Winning presentations* – The Learning Point Presentations School

- *The outstanding negotiator* – C. H. Godefroy and L Robert

I would like to say a special thank you to the Board Directors, Area Directors and Training Solutions department of the James McNaughton Paper Group.

They have given me the opportunity to write and deliver many sales training and development programmes over the past three years.

Julian Clay

About the author

Julian Clay has been successful in a sales role for nearly 20 years, first as a sales executive and then as a national account manager and sales director. In his last year as an account manager he was the top sales performer in Kodak's Office Imaging division in the UK. This gave him an invaluable insight into what makes sales people successful.

This led him to become a consultant in 1998. His first project involved finding a solution to common forecasting and account management issues. He developed sales models that help companies:

- Forecast future sales more accurately

- Develop and manage their accounts well

- Analyse the strengths and weaknesses of their sales performance

These have been used successfully by many companies and tailored to different markets. They enable a sale to be looked at in an objective way in order to improve performance and make someone more effective.

In 2001 he became a director of his own company, Sales 2 Success Limited, which also offers personalised sales development and coaching programmes. He has co-written a book on sales management.

Contents

About this book

Using self-assessment models, which Julian Clay has developed over many years, this book shows you how to track your progress in your own sales campaigns, how to identify where you may be going wrong and how to build a successful sales path of development.

Many books simply list prescribed techniques and leave the reader to interpret them. What make this book different is that it provides clear, practical advice on every aspect of making a sale, but you'll also find much more: templates, tables, exercises and stimulating ideas to develop your sales techniques and monitor your progress in a particular sale. Each chapter ends with a summary, key points and coaching advice on developing a particular part of the sales cycle.

If you've ever found yourself thinking 'I've done everything right, why haven't I got the sale?' this book is for you.

INTRODUCTION

Introduction

'*Successful Selling Solutions*' is aimed at people who have begun a career in sales as well as those who want to refresh themselves on some of the main issues. By developing a sale well, you stand a better chance of gaining genuine commitment and maintaining good profit margins.

It will also help middle and senior managers to have a better understanding of the sales process. Although each reader's market and level of experience will be different, many of the disciplines needed, will be the same.

We will introduce sales models to help you in three key areas:

- **Accurate forecasting**: To predict future sales and save you time

- **Account management**: To manage relationships/accounts more effectively

- **Sales performance**: To analyse and improve your own performance

The sales models introduced (in Chapters 1 and 10) will help you to develop a sale well. They can also be used for coaching purposes. You will be able to compare your perception with reality to become more objective at all stages of the sale.

By breaking down the sales cycle into parts and developing each one well you have more chance of success. This means that if you have a problem in a particular area, you will be in a better position to put it right. There are tables of information that you can tailor to your own needs. Most of them contain 'live' information to make them easier to interpret.

Progressing a sale well and gaining the right amount of commitment from a buyer will increase your chances of being successful. This will involve exceeding agreed sales targets which will allow you to earn commission /bonuses. This is the financial 'pay off' for all the hard work that is done in turning a prospect into a customer.

This book will enable you to develop a structured approach in order to make you more effective and this will help you to find your own successful selling solutions!

Factors that will affect your level of success

Today's selling environment

Changes in the marketplace, economy, communication and technology have had a big impact in the way companies buy their products and services. The development of the Internet and technology generally, has resulted in better communication and a faster pace at work. Salespeople need to adapt quickly to market trends, target account needs and expectations. Managing change remains a challenge to which good salespeople need to continually adapt.

Developing a sale well

Developing a sale properly makes it easier to focus on the best opportunities and use of your time. It is achieved by doing the right things at the right time in the right accounts. It will also involve you thinking of different alternatives to an issue. If one doesn't work you will need to think of and implement others. This will give you a better chance of winning a high proportion of the sales for which you aim.

Your determination to succeed

Desire to succeed, self-motivation and enthusiasm are some of the qualities that will help you achieve success. Other factors include patience, being a good listener and having good questioning skills. In the sales process you will make mistakes. Learn from them so that you minimise/eliminate them in the future.

Good salespeople are assertive, respecting other people's views as well as expecting the same in return. You will need to be pro-active with buyers and creative in your thinking. This will help you to manage different types of sales situation and illustrate to a buyer your determination to succeed.

Your selling style

You will need to consider how to develop your own selling style. By looking at your role and having a good understanding of your company and market you will increase your chances of applying your skills well. Your selling style will also affect how easily you adapt to a sales role.

A partnership approach

With many companies offering the same or similar products and services, it can be hard for customers to differentiate between suppliers. Some markets have a longer sales cycle (one year or more). Developing good business relationships can be a key factor in winning a sale and growing the account's potential.

This requires hard work, patience and skill. Having a partnership approach will make it easier to achieve this.

Being objective and taking responsibility

Good sales people look at a situation in an objective way and take responsibility for their part in managing the sales process. This maximises the chances of creating a good customer - supplier relationship.

Managing yourself, your targets and your time well

Being structured, flexible and disciplined will help you to manage yourself well. You will need to interpret your company's sales objectives by meeting/exceeding agreed sales targets and key performance indicators (K.P.I's). These should be agreed, easy to understand, fair and motivational.

There are only a limited number of sales opportunities in a day, week, month and year. Good time management will help you to prioritise on what is important to you. This includes deciding which accounts are worth spending time with and what business relationships to develop.

Your attitude

Having a positive attitude will help you maintain the right level of motivation. There are times when selling can be challenging and frustrating. Someone with a positive attitude who enjoys selling is more likely to succeed in this type of environment. Even if there are times when you don't feel highly motivated, a positive attitude can help focus your efforts.

Interpersonal skills and communication

In a sales role you need to develop good interpersonal skills. This will make it easier for buyers to relax and enable you to communicate well with them. Maintaining good eye contact and paying attention to their body language will help measure their true level of commitment at each stage of a sale.

Being persuasive

One of the main qualities that good sales people have is their ability to persuade. This involves:

- Understanding a target account's needs and looking for commitment

- Building trust when developing your business relationships

- Making the most of the time you have available

- Being consistent and determined

- Reinforcing that your products have value

These points will be easier to achieve if you have good selling skills and if you develop them. Being persuasive will mean that buyers will want to buy from you, as well as you wanting to sell to them!

The following table will enable you to find a personal route through the book. Topics have been selected that may be of particular interest to you. You may wish to refer to the chapter headings for an indication of the topics covered.

Topic reference table

Topic	Chapter	Pages
Managing the sales issues	1 Preparation and sales development, *(Recording sales call information)*	21
Accurate sales forecasting and coaching	1 Preparation and sales development, *(Forecasting future sales)*	27
Gaining maximum impact when writing to new accounts	2 Targeting new accounts, *(Written introduction techniques)*	50
Handling objections on the telephone	3 Telephone and personal introductions, *(Overcoming objections on the telephone)*	70
Ensuring that you have genuine commitment	4 Turning interest into commitment, *(Advanced questioning techniques)*	91
Linking your solution to the target account's need	5 Developing a sale correctly, *(Presenting the benefits of your solution)*	113

Topic	Chapter	Pages
Presenting the benefits of your solution	6 The presentation, *(Informal and formal presentations)*	136
Confirming the needs/pricing in writing to a target account	7 The sales proposal, *(Structuring a quotation and a proposal)*	154
Negotiating a 'win – win' situation	8 Negotiation, *(Bargaining and negotiation)*	175
Objection handling	9 Closing the sale, *(Buying signals and overcoming objections)*	200
Managing larger, more complex accounts	10 Managing your accounts and your performance, *(Developing an account strategy)*	224
Monitoring and developing your own performance	10 Managing your accounts and your sales perform-ance, *(Analysing your sales performance)*	235

Coaching

Coaching will help you to develop your selling skills. This can be done by looking at a sale that you are developing and breaking it down into a number of key areas, for example:

- What is the timescale?

- Who are your competitors?

- What is the target account's budget/level of spend?

At the end of a chapter each one of the coaching areas will be looked at in the form of a table, (see below). A question will be asked and you will get three possible answers, a negative, neutral or positive one. Choose the answer that best fits the current situation in that account. If you are not sure then find out, don't guess as this will affect your chances of getting a sale!

Depending on your answer, you will then get coaching advice. Creating your own model will help you to manage the different stages of a sale more effectively. This will ensure that you gain the right level of commitment in a number of areas before you close for an order.

This table forms part of the forecasting process and ten coaching areas are covered in more detail in Chapter 2 – Targeting new accounts, *(Developing a sale correctly and Forecasting future sales).*

Coaching table

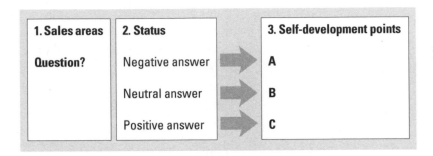

1. Sales areas	2. Status		3. Self-development points
Question?	Negative answer	→	A
	Neutral answer	→	B
	Positive answer	→	C

Glossary of sales terms

SALES TERM	MEANING
Target account	One that you are looking to do business with/develop a relationship with
Buyer	Decision-maker and often the budget holder(at middle/ senior management level)
Senior management	Board director (or in a plc – senior manager who a budget holder would report to)
Middle management	Reports to board director/ probably has 'manager' in job title. Probable decision-maker and budget holder in middle/large companies
Influencer	Someone who reports to a middle manager and has no budget/sole decision-making responsibility

Suspect	Someone who doesn't have a confirmed need but does buy your type of product/service
Prospect	Someone who has confirmed a need and buys your type of product/service
Customer	Someone who buys your product/service. Try to discover the length of the customer's buying cycle
Salesperson	Sales executive, account manager, sales consultant
Sales call	Appointment
'Would Like' need	'Interest' from a buyer/target account
'Must Have' need	'Commitment' from a buyer/target account
Quote	Short need/price confirmation
Proposal	More detailed need/price confirmation linking target account's needs to your solution
CRM – Customer Relationship Management	CRM looks at how companies can use knowledge about a target account's buying trends and people to communicate and serve them better. This will help to maximise growth and customer retention

We will refer to a company that you are looking to do business with as a 'target account' and the decision-maker in that account as the 'buyer'. A buyer could be at senior, middle or influencer level.

CHAPTER **ONE**

Preparation and sales development

Preparation and sales development

Introduction

Before you begin selling to any target account it is worth preparing yourself. This can involve knowing something about your market, your products and those of your competitors. By doing this, you will find it easier to manage each stage of a sale correctly. This can be made easier by having sales models in place to help you develop a sale well.

By the end of this chapter you will be able to:

- Identify the strengths and weaknesses of your products/ services.

- Prepare good call objectives and record the right type of information.

- Define the relevant stages of your sales cycle.

- Forecast future business accurately.

This will make it easier to manage each stage of a sale.

Your products and your competitors

Knowing your products and services well, how they compare with your competitors and their strengths and weakness, is part of the preparation process.

Preparation

As you target new and existing accounts there are two key areas in which you should continually update yourself. These are the strengths and weaknesses of:

1   your company and the products/services you sell; and

2   your competitors and the products/services they sell.

This knowledge will gain you credibility in the eyes of a buyer. It will give you confidence that you are offering the right solution when you get a requirement. Filling in a simple table can suffice comparing your company with your competitors *(see overleaf)*.

Competition – Strengths and weaknesses

Company	Strengths	Weaknesses
Your company	• Good product range • Our service is perceived as very good • National distribution network	• No history in the account • Don't know buyer very well • Company A have good and long-standing relationship
Competitor A	• Good and long relationship • National distribution network • Specialised IT offering	• Limited product range • Perceived as expensive
Competitor B	• Perceived as good value for money • Local service	• Don't have national distribution network • After sales service • Poor relationship history

Competitor C	• Good product range	• Reliability
	• Special IT offering	• After sales service
	• Flexible offers	
	• Relationship building	

Although many salespeople know much of this information, it is easier to be objective when it is written down and monitored. With the introduction of customer relationship management (CRM) and contact databases, companies have the ability to attach this on their Intranet to a prospect/customer record. Or it can be stored in a central sales development file.

Other valuable information to know and update is your product/ service offering compared with the competition. Many buyers will expect you to know this. Once again this can be illustrated in the form of a table *(see overleaf)*.

A table like this is a good reminder of what a competitor is likely to offer against you when comparing a number of your different product offerings.

By being aware of the products/services you sell you will gain knowledge. This will impress buyers and help to confirm your company's strengths and product offers. It will also help you to be better prepared to know how to counter a competitor's solution.

Product strengths versus competition

Your product/ service	Your strengths		Main competition	Product	Their strengths
W	• Brand awareness • Reliability	>	Company A	Product A	• Good value for money • Reliability
X	• Flexible pricing • Up-to-date product	>	Company B	Product B	• Well known • Reliable
Y	• Well known • Reliable • Market leader • Good value	>	Company C	Product C	• Flexible pricing • Good history of reliability
Z	• New/exciting • Durable	>	Company D	Product D	• Market leader • Good history of reliability

Recording sales-call information

Another way of preparing well is to ensure that you ask the right questions in a call and record the right type of information. By doing this you will increase your chances of developing the sale properly and keep the buyer's interest. Getting the correct information will also help you turn interest into commitment more easily.

Call objectives – questioning areas

When you look to sell a product or service it is worth considering what areas target accounts buy in and their buying cycle/frequency. What criteria do they have? Knowing this will help you to focus on the areas of added value. The ones that you should consider exploring when you go into a target account for the first time, or you are developing an existing account, include:

THE SALES ISSUES

1 View of your company

2 View of your main competitors

3 Your products/services

4 After sales service

5 Account management/business relationship needs

6 Value for money

For nearly all companies, these are **the sales issues!**

This information is what target accounts make their buying decisions on. These areas are also the ones where any objections might come at the end of a sale, if a buyer has any. (This is looked at in more detail in Chapter 8 – Negotiation, (*Setting out your objectives*). You should consider finding out a buyer's attitude in all of the sales issue areas even if he/she has a definite requirement.

Look at a target account in detail. You want to ensure that you look at the areas where you are strong as well as where you are weaker. If a buyer has a requirement, his/her interest can still be affected in some of the other areas, especially if there is little to choose between you and another supplier. By checking the buyer's attitude to these six areas you increase your chances of covering the buying criteria well.

Discussing prices early on in a sale can focus a buyer away from the other 'added value' areas. By looking at other sales issues you will have more chance of understanding why a target account has chosen another supplier (if they are not a customer of yours). Once buyers have focused on price they can be less interested in other elements your offer, unless it is to match/beat their current supplier.

Buyers who only buy on price tend not to be loyal and rarely give you good profit margin potential. However, questions on pricing must not be confused with ones about good value for money.

You can create your own call objectives table, with common 'added value' questions in the different sales issue areas. It allows you to tailor your questions to different types of account, depending on what information you want to find out. In the following example, we have picked three of the six sales issue areas:

- *In the left hand column* we have added a list of questions related to the sales issue.

- *In the right hand column* are examples of how you can personalise your own questions.

This will help to focus your attention on what issues to discuss with a buyer.

Sales issues table – call objectives

Questioning Areas	Account Mgr: Steve Nolan
Account: ABC Limited – Sue Saville	
Pre-call notes: Main questioning areas	

1 VIEW OF YOUR COMPANY

a) Current awareness/view of your company?

b) Why haven't they used your products before?

c) If so why did they stop using you?

d) Attitude towards your products?

e) Key needs from their supplier?

f) Future developments in your company?

POINTS TO COVER

- Haven't used us before, what is their market knowledge?

- Did they have a bad experience/referral?

2 VIEW OF THE COMPETITION

a) Current suppliers and their relationships?

b) View of their competition?

c) Competitor favoured products/services?

d) Why do they use competition?

e) Reasons for using them?

f) History with them?

POINTS TO COVER

- What do they look for and what relationship do they want?

- Why are they so supportive of our main competitor?

3 PRODUCTS AND SERVICES

  a) Existing product/service requirements?

  b) What are they looking for in the future?

  c) Current levels of expectation?

  d) Do they have need, budget and approval?

  e) Is there a timeframe to work to?

  f) Product and service experience?

POINTS TO COVER

- Is there a timeframe to replace current technology?

A table like this can be used for any type of appointment, not only first appointments. Creating one is a good discipline to get into and can help you ask the right questions, which is the key to getting the right type of information.

Call structure and visits

In preparation for an appointment and as part of your call structure, arrive at a target account's offices at least fifteen minutes before the appointment. This will enable you allow for any travel problems that could arise. It will give you time to focus on what areas you intend to cover as part of your call objectives.

In any sales call you should look to have some type of agenda, even if it is not written down. This will make it easier for a buyer to understand the need for the call and the need for him/her to answer questions. Some companies have this written down in a formal manner. For example:

- Introduce yourself/your company/your sales role.

- Explain why you are making this visit.

- Ask if it is alright to ask questions and record information (written, not on a laptop, as this can be off-putting for a buyer).

- Confirm what has been agreed.

- Focus on next steps – (agree who will do what by when).

- Get commitment from a buyer – for next meeting.

- Agree a timeframe and possible agenda.

This simple process can help you to be structured, which in turn will look professional and makes it easier for a buyer to follow. It also commits a buyer to 'next steps' in the sales process!

When you have finished the appointment you should spend time reviewing it and making any additional notes while the sales information is fresh in your mind. This preparation and review process will help you to maximise your effectiveness in sales appointments.

Recording relevant information will help you develop a sale correctly. By focusing your questioning in the sales issue areas you will have more chance of covering a target account's needs. This will take the focus away from product and price only. It will also help to differentiate you from your competitors and give a buyer confidence in you.

Forecasting future sales

Another aspect of being well prepared is to look at the way you develop a sale and forecast future business. If this is done well it will make it easier for you to define a need and turn any interest you have into commitment. (We will look at this area in more detail in Chapter 4 – Turning interest into commitment). Reducing the time spent in target accounts where you are unlikely to win any business will improve your level of effectiveness.

Salespeople tend to be optimistic by nature. This is a positive trait, but it can lead to over-optimism. You can counter this by measuring your perception against reality and having accurate information to help you. This will increase your chances of making the most of your sales opportunities.

Why forecast?

Accurate forecasting can help companies to manage their sales well and plan with confidence. It will give you (whether you are a Director/Manager or Sales Executive), a better understanding of what steps need to be taken when developing a sale. This can be developed into a forecasting model.

There are a number of factors that affect the accuracy of forecasting future sales and we will deal with these individually. An essential part of this will be to ensure that anyone wishing to employ the process sees the benefits of using a model. By creating one you will save time, prioritise and manage the closing stages of the sale well. It can also be a vital part in any company's CRM (customer relationship management) programme, as your business will rely on a number of sales being won.

You will need to take time and care in completing a model. It won't take long and the benefit will be much more time saved later, if sales are not being developed well. Before you create your own model, consider your own position in a target account by:

- Identifying that an account is actually worth doing business with.

- Ensuring 'key players' have confirmed a timeframe.

- Listing the stages the account is going through as a sale is developed.

- Listing the account's buying criteria and ensuring that the needs are met.

- Confirming the budget/spend.

You will then need to define a worse, average and best case scenario of possible outcomes. This will help you to compare where you are with where you need to be! Another factor to take into account is whether you are selling a 'one off' product, a service, repeat business or through indirect channels.

We will now look at other issues that need to be identified in order to build an accurate forecasting model.

Forecasting issues

Other issues that can affect the accuracy of a forecast and the 'buy in' from a sales executive include:

- The balance between optimism and realism. A forecasting model might reveal that you have less business coming in than you should have!

- Communication/contact with different levels of management in a target account.

- Short selling time-frames (a matter of days) or repeat business, as this can make accurate forecasting more difficult to predict.

- Lack of awareness/experience – Salespeople may be unsure of the steps involved in making a forecast or may not develop them correctly!

- Timeframe! This is perhaps the most important element in forecasting a sale.

Let us now look at the 'timeframe' element before we develop our own model.

Timeframe

For any forecasting model to work properly it must have a confirmed timeframe. Without being realistic, you are in danger of having the same accounts appearing on your forecast list, month after month.

The accuracy of the timeframe will be affected by:

- Someone not qualifying the needs of the target account properly.

- Someone not understanding their buying cycle.

- Circumstances/buying criteria changing.

- Internal changes that could triggered by demand/economic factors, a merger, company strategy etc.

Factors affecting a target account's timeframe should be taken into account when a forecast is predicted. To help you, let us now define short-term and long-term forecasting.

Short-term and long-term forecasting

For the purpose of this section, a timeframe of one month will be used to describe short-term forecasting. For long-term forecasting we will assume three to six months ahead.

It is harder to predict longer-term business because not all sales issues will have been discussed, properly developed or resolved. These become clearer as the sale progresses. It is still important to develop long-term prospects so that you have an opportunity to influence their buying criteria. Let us now look at the criteria needed for us to create a forecasting model.

Criteria to use in a model

The most common issues that will affect the accuracy of a forecasting model include:

1 Timescale.

2 Competition.

3 Spend.

4 Solution.

5 Commitment.

6 Presentation.

7 Proposals.

8 Negotiation.

9 Close.

10 Internal barriers.

There are other issues that you could include. However, in this model we will use ten areas. The next stage is to turn these into ten questions. For example:

• What is the confirmed timescale etc?

You can then list the other nine areas to complete the questions needed in the forecasting table.

Knowing your own sales cycle as well as your target account can help you to break it down. This will ensure that you cover each stage correctly and get back into the cycle if a situation changes. We can now begin the process of building a model.

Forecast grading

You can now grade each of your ten questions in the following way:

1 A 'worse case' scenario scores **0**

2 Issues that are partly solved but where there are still some actions needing to be completed score **5**

3 Where you have totally satisfied the criteria of the target account in any of the ten categories scores **10**

You are now ready to complete your own table! You should do one that has been agreed at every level of your management and which is common to each user. This will avoid confusion and ensure that every relevant person understands it.

Forecast table

Account: ? **Account Manager:** ? **Date:** ?

New or existing account: New **Product solution:** ? **Revenue:** £ **Profit:** £

Rating	Timescale - What is the confirmed time-scale?	Competition?	Spend?	Solution?	Commitment?	Presentation?	Proposal?	Negotiation?	Close date?	Barriers?
	(0 - 10)	(0 - 10)	(0 - 10)	(0 - 10)	(0 - 10)	(0 - 10)	(0 - 10)	(0 - 10)	(0 - 10)	(0 - 10)
0%	There is no definite timescale agreed yet or I don't know if it will be this month	Negative status	Negative status	Negative status	Negative status	Negative status	Negative status	Negative status	Negative status	Negative status
5%	Timescale should be this month, but this has yet to be confirmed by the Decision-Maker & Senior Mgt	Neutral status	Neutral status	Neutral status	Neutral status	Neutral status	Neutral status	Neutral status	Neutral status	Neutral status
10%*	Timescale has been confirmed by the Decision-Maker and Senior Management as this month	Positive status	Positive status	Positive status	Positive status	Positive status	Positive status	Positive status	Positive status	Positive status
Your score	5%	Column score %	Column score %	Column score %	Column score %	Column score %	Column score %	Column score %	Column score %	Column score % = 5%

Senior management = **Directors** - (Managing, sales, finance, production, marketing, purchasing + chief executive - Delegates authority to Middle management
Middle management = **Managers** - (Facilities, Purchasing, Training, IT etc. - Probable Decision-Maker/controller of a budget)
Influencers = **Assistant** - (supervisor, office services manage, Assistant - non budget holder)

Below 50% = Not a current prospect for this quarter
50 – 75% = Quarterly prospect (or will only buy on price)
75%+ = Should be a confirmed order this month

* Any score in excess of 75% should have timescale score of 10!

Forecast table

A final table will illustrate the row of ten questions you will have created, along with the grading from 0 – 10 for each question. At the bottom of each column your score for each question is added. In the final column and bottom row of the table, your total score as a percentage is calculated.

Below the table, a prediction of the likely outcome (at that time) is seen, depending you're your score. You will note that a definition of different levels of management is also shown. This is done because your forecast is more likely to be accurate if all levels of management have agreed it. Whatever, score you have (unless it is 100%), you will have areas on which to focus to develop the sales properly.

Note that there is a contradiction if you are predicting a sale this month, but your timescale score is only 5! To overcome this, any score in excess of 75% should have timescale score of 10!

You can now create a table combining your list of prospects with their forecast score. This will help you to prioritise which accounts need the most development.

The forecasting scores are most effective when:

- You provide accurate information.
- You understand the need to forecast accurately.
- The process is understood, implemented and supported by the senior and middle management levels of the company.

You can now create a table combining your list of prospects with their forecast score. This will help you to prioritise on which accounts need the most development.

Monthly sales forecast

	Prospect	New or existing?	Solution	Revenue (Units)	Gross profit (Units)	%	Closing appointment date
1.	Company A	N	X	4,500	900	90%	10th
2.	Company B	E	X	4,400	880	80%	29th
3.	Company C	E	X	4,700	940	80%	17th
4.	Company D	N	X	4,550	910	75%	22nd
5.	Company E	N	X	16,550	3,310	70%	Next month
6.	Company F	N	X	16,775	3,355	70%	20th
7.	Company G	E	X	17,000	3,400	70%	No
8.	Company H	E	X	16,000	3,200	70%	28th
9.	Company I	E	Y	3,500	700	60%	No
10.	Company J	N	Y	3,225	645	60%	Next month
11.	Company K	N	Y	2,995	599	55%	Next month
12.	Company L	N	Z	4,500	900	50%	No
13.	Company M	E	Z	3,995	799	45%	No
14.							
15.							
16.							
17.							
18.							
19.							
20.							
			Total	102,690	20,538		

Below 50% = Not a current prospect for this quarter
50 – 75% = Quarterly prospect (or will only buy on price)
75%+ = Should be a confirmed order this month

75%+ - should be a confirmed order

* Any score in excess of 75% should have timescale score of 10!

This table would normally be used as summary of a number of accounts being forecast in one quarterly period. You can also use it to highlight/prioritise accounts and show scores in a certain percentage band (over 75% for example).

You will notice that there is a column that asks you to confirm whether you have a closing appointment and if so, when? This is so that, if you have confirmed a sale this month, you should also know when the sale is due to be closed. Your forecasting accuracy will be affected if you continually score over 75% but have no firm date for the order to be closed!

Let us now look at areas that can be addressed if you find that your prediction does not match up with what actually happens!

Troubleshooting

Sometimes, a percentage score does not match the outcome. For example:

1   *You have a score of over 75% and a sale was delayed or lost!* This can be caused by:

   • Changes in the account's circumstances.

   • The information you put in the forecast model being inaccurate or too subjective!

   • The type of questions that have been asked.

   • A target account having a very good relationship with a competitor!

   • The sale not being developed correctly.

2   *You have scored under 50%, yet managed to close the order within the month!* This can be caused by:

- A target account buying mainly on price rather than value.

- The buying cycle being shortened.

- A buyer being imposed with a deadline.

3   *Monthly prospects appear again and again!* This can be caused by:

- Being over-optimistic.

- You not being thorough/knowing enough about the target account's needs.

- Not 'buying in' to the forecasting model!

A common reason for all three situations occurring can be you not knowing enough about the account's overall buying/decision-making process!

If your answer to a question falls to one of two choices, *choose the lower scoring one!* This will help you increase your forecasting accuracy. You should also check that your prediction matches the outcome so that your understanding of the account's position is accurate.

When you get an order, leave the score as it was on the day you got it, for self-development purposes. For example, the score was 85% and the reason it wasn't 100% was that you scored 5, not 10, in three of the ten areas. If this happens you should look at whether this is a pattern that happens in other accounts. If it is, then you should consider how to develop yourself in these areas.

Other sales models

There are other types of sales model you can use to manage target accounts and sales opportunities:

1 Forecast tracking

If you supply fast-selling goods that have a low individual price, you can predict a monthly sales figure based on daily sales to the target account. This can be done in two ways:

1. *Look at the monthly revenue/profit potential as a whole, not individual products.* This will allow you to check that you have covered the range of forecasting issues well.

2. *Use another forecasting method – Forecast tracking.* Daily forecast tracking can be used to compare what someone has done (at any given point in a month) and what sales he/she would achieve if they continued at the current daily sales level. This can be updated daily and can help focus your efforts.

If someone is behind the monthly target, he/she can contact a target account to find out why sales are falling below a predicted level. This gives you a chance to contact the account as soon as a downturn occurs, which will help you to correct the situation.

2 Compatibility table

You can create a set of criteria to compare how compatible target accounts are with your company. This will help you prioritise which ones have the most partnership potential. This is done in the same way in which a forecasting model was created and is illustrated in Chapter 10 – Managing your accounts and your performance, (*Developing an account strategy*).

These methods offer you flexibility to look at a target account in a number of different ways. By creating your own models, you can compare where you are with where you want to be in the target account. It will help you prioritise which accounts to develop and what issues to discuss to develop a sale well.

Accurate forecasting is about managing the stages of a sale well in a number of areas. If this is done, you stand a better chance of winning more business. You will make the most effective use of your time by focusing on the best sales opportunities.

Chapter summary

In this chapter we have looked at:

- Your products and your competitors.
- Recording sales call information.
- Forecasting future sales.

Good preparation is an investment of your time. Lost sales and the time spent on target accounts that produce little/no business have a cost attached. Improving your effectiveness by being well prepared will help you focus on the sales issues and the right accounts. It will also improve your time management skills and help you to build good relationships with the right people.

Having a way of developing a sale properly will improve your chances of winning more business. Creating a forecasting model is a way of achieving this and sharing it internally. This will improve your communication of the sales issues to colleagues who are involved in the sales process.

Key points

✓ Know your key products strengths and weaknesses (and those of your competitors'!).

✓ Be aware of what the competition will offer against you.

✓ Remember that target accounts buy on a number of issues.

✓ Use relevant sales models to help you.

✓ Be objective – Compare your perception with reality!

Coaching table

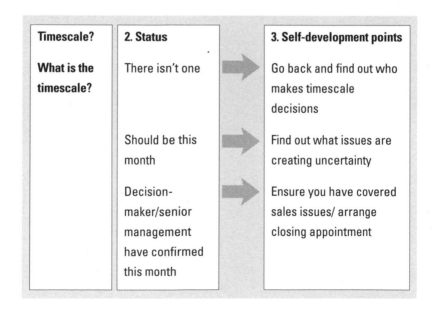

Timescale?	2. Status		3. Self-development points
What is the timescale?	There isn't one	→	Go back and find out who makes timescale decisions
	Should be this month	→	Find out what issues are creating uncertainty
	Decision-maker/senior management have confirmed this month	→	Ensure you have covered sales issues/ arrange closing appointment

CHAPTER **TWO**

Targeting new accounts

Targeting new accounts

Introduction

Knowing about your products, your competitors and having a forecasting model to help you develop a sale will make it easier to target new accounts – breaking into new accounts is harder than maintaining existing ones. Acquiring this knowledge will make it easier to build new business relationships.

By the end of this chapter you will be able to:

- Know what information you need to begin a dialogue in a new account.

- Distinguish your company from its competitors.

- Write professional introductions (by letter or email).

Introducing yourself to a new account is the beginning of the business relationship. If this goes well, it will give you greater opportunities to sell into and grow the account.

Background information on a target account

Having good information about a target account before you meet a buyer will help to build your credibility, confidence and knowledge. To do this you will need to find out something about the account.

What information do you need?

Some of the information you will need to find out should include something about the target account's:

- products and services;
- company history;
- competitors;
- turnover and profit;
- current challenges;
- core business objectives;
- strategic direction;
- company structure; and
- buying cycle/behaviour/attitude.

With this knowledge, you will show buyers respect and make it easier to begin a dialogue with them. Most of the information listed above can be found in:

1 A company's annual report.

2 A company's sales literature.

3 On the Internet.

It can take time to learn about your target accounts, but it will help you to develop a good understanding of the account. You will need to decide which ones to spend time researching. A company's annual report and accounts will give a greater insight into their products, services and most importantly – their culture! It will help you to know how much value they put on the products and services you sell. This has a number of benefits. It will enable you to:

- Assess the account's potential.

- Develop a good/better relationship with the buyer/decision-maker.

- Decide how much to spend pursuing the account.

- Differentiate yourself against your competitors.

The effort you put in has to be compared with the results you get. By doing this you can assess the value of the time spent on each account. You can also look at the type of relationship you have with each account contact. This will help to ensure that your relationship develops in the way you want it to!

Linking your company's benefits with a target account

When you first meet someone in a target account it is a good idea to discuss any stated goals/intentions/policies that they have. This will help to give contacts the impression that you are interested in them and their company. You can then look to link the benefits your company has to offer with the target account information. You can create a table that looks at linking this with your own company's benefits. For example:

Target account report information	Benefit links with your company
1 Group *commitment* to deliver 'added value services'	We also look at best *value for money* services to customers
2 Key business driver is gaining a *competitive advantage*	Our key business drivers are: Growth by looking at *innovative ways of gaining impact* in the marketplace
3 *Customer satisfaction* 'is our primary goal' – Chairman	We are dedicated to ensure that we have a thorough *understanding of our customers needs and then producing effective value-for-money solutions*
4 Be selective in *choosing the right business partners*	Our long-term strategy is to work with companies that can be supported properly by us and where we can *add value* to their business
5 To maintain and grow our existing customer base and *support the new products coming* out this year	We look at controlled growth to ensure that we can *support new products and services* effectively
6 To *maintain professional standards* and ethics throughout the group	We have a long *history of high professional standards,* code of conduct and after sales service

7	To continue to *expand* in existing market sectors	We are growing, and introducing new software products to *help companies grow their business more effectively*
8	To continue to *build up business relationships* with some of our top suppliers	We have some customers who have dealt with us for over 20 years. *Building strong business relationships* is part of our strategy

The level of contact you meet and their role in the company will affect what you include in your agenda.

Many buyers at influencer and middle management level get used to salespeople wanting to ask questions about product requirements straight away. Knowing something about a target account (providing it is not of low value potential) can help to distinguish you from your competitors. It will also show the person you meet that you have a consultative and business-like approach.

Differentiating yourself from your competitors

Another aspect of targeting new accounts is to look at what selling points you have that distinguish your company from others. Most buyers that you meet for the first time will be thinking, "Why should we buy from you?"

Distinguishing selling points

Every company looks at ways of differentiating themselves by having unique selling points – U.S.P.'s. Today, this definition is very hard to live up to. Perhaps *distinguishing selling points* would be a better term. This is because there are very few companies that can boast a unique advantage in the marketplace.

PRACTICAL POINTER

Look at your own D.S.P.'s. This will help you gain confidence in your products and services and make you better prepared

The areas at which you will look to establish an advantage over your competitors are the 'Sales Issues in Chapter One – Preparation and sales development, (*Recording sales call information*), i.e. View of your company, view of your main competitors, your products/services

Once again this can be illustrated in a table. You can then refer to it and use it to show a buyer that you have given thought to the different areas in which he/she will make their buying decisions.

Your Distinguishing Selling Point areas

VIEW OF YOUR COMPANY:

- Trading for over twenty years – seen as a product leader by many customers

- Good customer base – some good long-standing relationships

- Strength of our people – investment in their development

VIEW OF THE COMPETITION:

- We have the best reputation for service

- We are a leader in the field, compared with some of our rivals

- We have invested proportionately more in R & D than many of our competitors

PRODUCTS/SERVICES:

- Our main product range is the most reliable on the market

- Our new range of hardware has cut down-time in the IT department by over 20%

- We have a reputation for innovative products

AFTER SALES SERVICE/SUPPORT:

- Industry leader

- We have good after-sales reputation – customer care focus

- We offer a three year guarantee on products – compared with industry's two year standard

ACCOUNT MANAGEMENT/BUSINESS RELATIONSHIP NEEDS:

- We place a high priority on training, self-development and customer focus
- Many of our business relationships have been in place for many years
- We have an established code of conduct
- We have many experienced and successful account managers

VALUE FOR MONEY:

- We offer many value-for-money/high-value solutions
- We won last year's prestigious 'product of the year' award
- Our customers can confirm that we offer very good value for money

OTHER D.S.P'S:

- Recently won top marketing award for innovation
- Our products in the UK market have grown faster than any of our competitors

A strategy like this is useful when you are at the negotiating stage with a company. When you link your solution to a buyer's need you can reinforce the value of your company's distinguishing selling points. This will be looked at in 'Chapter 8 – Negotiation, (*Setting out your objectives*).

Having done some research on a target account, and knowing the points that distinguish your company from others, will give you confidence and make you look professional. It will also make it easier to manage the next step in the sales cycle – personal introductions!

Written introduction techniques

Perhaps the biggest challenge of any salesperson's search for business is to gain new customers. One of the most effective ways of doing this is to write an introduction letter, followed up by a telephone call. (Cold calling is covered in Chapter 3 – Telephone and personal introductions, (*Cold calling on the telephone*)).

We will look at how you can structure simple letters to maximise the chances of gaining a first appointment.

Written introductions

Written introduction are a good way of developing a new business relationship with a target account. This can be done with a:

- letter;
- mail shot;
- promotion; or by
- email.

This can then be followed up with a phone call to try to get an appointment to see the relevant person in the target company.

A **mail shot**, tends to be sent out to a high number of target accounts (perhaps over one hundred – where the buyer may not even be known). Another way of contacting target accounts is to do a product **promotion**. You might have a special price for a limited period of time on selected products. Sending a buyer an **email** is another form of quick, easy communication. But it can easily be deleted and some buyers might see it as intrusive.

The answer is to experiment and look at your own market and your company's products to define the best way to target new accounts. Although any written introduction will have limited value if you expect a buyer to contact you at this stage of the sales process!

We will now go on to look at written introductions in more detail.

Introduction and benefit

The purpose of using an introductory letter can be two-fold:

1   It is a way of getting you and your company known to a target account.

2   It gives you reason to contact a buyer to arrange a first appointment.

A good introductory letter looks professional and makes it easier for you to begin a dialogue with a buyer. There are four key elements to an introductory letter:

1   **Hook**
Something to get the person's interest

2   **Personal and brief company introduction**
What you do and for whom you work for – what's in it for them?

3   **Benefit/proof statement + references (optional)**
Reason for wanting a meeting

4   **Close**

When you write a letter be aware of the job role of the person you are targeting. A Director looks at the strategic situation, so be brief. Middle Management looks at the overall picture and would need a more detail of the benefit, related to his/her area of responsibility. This level of management is most likely to control a budget and be the decision-maker. Someone who influences a sale, but has no direct authority to buy, tends to be more product- and service-related.

If you put too much product or company information in an introductory letter there is a danger that you start to sound like everybody else. "Hello, my name is.............. and I work for the 3rd largest software supplier of X in the UK". Without a direct benefit to the recipient, be careful that he/she can't read your letter and think – 'so what'!

PRACTICAL POINTER

Remember not to include a product solution directly in your letter. You can't solve someone's issues or fulfil their requirements if you don't know what they are or if you haven't met the decision-maker/buyer!

You are looking to introduce yourself and your company, *NOT* sell them something directly through your letter (unless it is a promotional one)! Primarily, the objective is to get a first appointment!

Introductory letters can be effective if you manage to get the person's attention in the first paragraph. This is difficult, so you will need to focus on common issues that affect his/her job role and keep the letter brief. Also, ensure that you look at the situation from the recipient's point of view to try to establish what common issues might be top of his/her agenda. This will help you to get a first appointment and build a good rapport with that person.

We will now look at two different types of introductory letter. The first will have bullet points as a hook; the second will be written as a normal paragraph. For a first letter it is probably better to use someone's surname rather than first name. This can be dependent on the type of market you are in, but it is polite to begin in this way if you don't know that person.

Addressing the letter is made more difficult when you are writing to a lady buyer who might be Mrs, Miss or Ms. In this case; it is advisable to find out what your contact prefers to be known as (without speaking to that person directly). It is good business practice to address contacts with their initials and job title (or business qualification), for example:

Date:

Mr T Ronson BSc
Production Director
Stockwell Controls Limited
1 Drapers Lane
London
SW9 1AE

You should also look at limiting the name and address to five/six lines so that it can be clearly seen in a window envelope. Put the date above the name and address. Also, always ask your existing customers if they mind you using their name as a reference!

Examples of introductory letters

Example 1

Introductory letter to Mr T Ronson – Production Director of a packaging company.

Date:

Mr T Ronson BSc
Production Director
Stockwell Controls Limited
1 Drapers Lane
London
SW9 1AE

Dear Mr Ronson

Hook: As the head of production in your company, I'm sure that you'll be looking at issues such as:

- How can I best rationalise my annual spend?

- How can I best manage the control of my stock levels?

- Can any more be done to improve production levels?

- How can I get more value for money without losing quality?

Personal/Co. Introduction: I am an account manager for Inventory Management Limited. We specialise in helping companies solve these types of issues.

Benefit: The reason for contacting you is that many buyers have found that they have been able to improve their overall production efficiency by working in partnership with us.

Optional: This has been due to our success in helping to better manage stock control and inventory levels.

Optional: Some examples include Company D and Company E who have seen considerable productivity improvements since working in partnership with us.

Close: I will contact you in the next few days to arrange a mutually convenient appointment.

Yours sincerely,

John Simmons
Account Manager – South
Email:jsimmons@iml.com
Mobile: 07711 100100

Example 2

Introduction letter to Mrs S Partoni – IT Manager of an Insurance company.

Date:

Mrs S Partoni
IT Manager
Insure Limited
66 Bury Lane
Manchester
MR1 ZBD

Dear Mrs Partoni

Hook: There is currently much competition in the insurance industry to look at new ways to manage customer data in the event of a disaster.

Company benefit: We specialise in helping companies manage their customer data in a pro-active way to prevent loss of information in the event of a network breakdown.

Industry benefit: As a supplier of 'disaster recovery' software I would like to discuss the difference it has made to our customers. A recent 'Insurance Monthly' survey said that this type of software improved business performance by more than 12%.

I will contact you in the next few days to arrange
a meeting.

Yours sincerely,

Jane Byford
Account Manager – North
Email:jbyford@abc.co.uk
Mobile: 07711 200200

The main points to remember in an introductory letter are to:

- Have a good reason to write one.

- Have a structure.

- Do some research on the account first (but don't include too much information).

- Experiment until you get one you like (and that is effective).

- Expect some level of rejection as well as success – and target yourself on this.

- Focus on what the target account will gain from a meeting with you!

Introductory letters are a good discipline and encourage you to prospect for new business. They have an advantage over a 'cold call' in that the recipient will know why you want to come and see them, the nature of your role and something about your company. This will increase your chances of being successful in a follow up telephone call leading to an appointment.

Chapter summary

In this chapter we have looked at:

- Background information on a target account.

- Differentiating yourself from your competitors.

- Written introduction techniques.

Targeting new accounts is a vital part of the new-business process. How you do this can set the tone for the way a business relationship develops. The amount of preparation work you do will depend on the type of account you are targeting, your knowledge of the account and the value of the products and services you sell. By doing this you stand a better chance of differentiating yourself from your competitors.

Although this work can take time, it will give you to have a better understanding of the target account. Written introductions will help you get a first appointment with a buyer.

Key points

✓ Take time to find out some background information on a target account.

✓ Understand and focus on what your 'Distinguishing Selling Points' are.

✓ Remember to structure an introductory letter/email.

✓ Use a letter to get an introduction/appointment (not to do the selling for you)!

Coaching table

1. Competition?	2. Status		3. Self-development points
Are you preferred to the competition?	No/not sure	→	Find out why and what the competition can do that you can't
	The target account is neutral/has no preferred choice	→	Focus the account on their buying criteria and link this to your solution/ D.S.P's
	You are the preferred choice/there is no competition	→	Get commitment so that the target account doesn't feel the need to look elsewhere

CHAPTER **THREE**

Telephone and personal introductions

Telephone and personal introductions

Key questions

The next stage, if you have written an introductory letter, is to follow it up with a phone call. If you have chosen to do a 'cold call' instead, you will need to have a good reason in order to gain a buyer's interest.

By the end of this chapter you will be able to:

- Motivate yourself to achieve a realistic number of sales appointments.

- Have a structure to make it easier to introduce yourself on the telephone.

- Overcome some of the most common telephone objections.

- Create good first impression in an appointment.

Meeting buyers for the first time is challenging. If you create a good impression on the telephone and then in person, you will get their attention. This will make it easier to develop any sales opportunities.

Introductory telephone techniques

Being prepared before you make an introduction by telephone can improve your success rate. For a buyer, this could be the first time he/she has ever spoken to someone from your company. Let us look at what you can do to maximize your chances of getting an appointment and to maintain your levels of motivation.

Ten 'tips' when introducing yourself on the telephone

1 BE REALISTIC ABOUT YOUR SUCCESS RATE

Before you start telephoning a target account (whether it be cold or as a follow up to a letter or email), set yourself a realistic target of appointments. For example, for every ten calls try to get four appointments. This will help to improve your 'hit rate'.

If you do not achieve your target then look at the reasons why. Are you:

- Targeting the right person?
- Feeling positive enough?
- Saying the right thing?
- Speaking clearly?
- Prepared?

These are all factors that will affect your success rate.

2 DON'T TAKE ANY REJECTION PERSONALLY

Nobody likes being rejected and this is understandable. A positive trait of many salespeople is the need to be liked. If a buyer rejects the opportunity to even begin a dialogue, this can be taken personally. Don't let this happen, instead see rejection as part of the new business targeting process.

3 DON'T FOLLOW A WRITTEN SCRIPT

You should have a good idea of what you are going to say to a buyer. Write down bullet points to support this but don't read a script. If you do it will sound unconvincing and false. It will lessen your chances of getting a first appointment.

4 HAVE YOUR TARGET ACCOUNT INFORMATION PREPARED

When you are about to telephone a target account, remember to have any relevant background information available to refer to. This will give the buyer confidence in you.

5 BE PREPARED FOR A BUYER'S REACTION

Being prepared for a buyer's reaction to your request for an appointment will make it easier to overcome any possible objections. We will look at overcoming common telephone objections in this chapter, (*Overcoming objections on the telephone*).

6 KEEP CALLS BRIEF AND BUSINESS-LIKE

Unless you have a Tele-sales/marketing role your objective is to get a face-to-face appointment – not to sell your products on the telephone! Keep the calls brief and 'to the point' as this will give you a stronger basis for a discussion at a first meeting.

7 DON'T' GET INTO SPECIFICS!

Don't go into too much detail about your products/services or offer a possible solution. By doing this you give the buyer a stronger reason not to see you in person. This can be hard, especially where a buyer is interested or you feel that you have a solution to a particular issue.

8 SET ASIDE A REGULAR TIME ON A PARTICULAR DAY/WEEK

By getting into a routine you will increase your chances of gaining new appointments. Try to set aside a regular date and time to do this and only do a set number in one go – perhaps twenty. Choose a time when you are at your best. Don't be distracted or redirected by other sales issues that you have to do. Let colleagues know that you would like their help in not being interrupted during this time.

9 DON'T GET INVOLVED IN AN ARGUMENT WITH SOMEONE!

If you find that a buyer does not want to see you, or provokes you in some way, don't get involved in an argument! Thank that person politely for his/her time and move on to the next call. Don't take it personally or let it de-motivate you!

10 BE POSITIVE

If you feel confident you will convey this to a buyer. If you sound interesting and positive, this will have a positive effect on the person receiving the call. However, if a buyer says no three times to you, find out why and then move on to the next call. Try and get agreement from a buyer to 'phone them back in a few weeks time and note this.

Good telephone techniques are important because they come at the beginning of a sales cycle. If you can get to the next stage successfully, you at least have the chance to meet a buyer and build an understanding of his situation. The next step is what to say in a 'cold call' or a 'follow up call' to a written letter or email.

Cold calling on the telephone

Speaking to a buyer for the first time on the telephone will involve you being prepared and in the right frame of mind. This can be made easier if you have written an introductory letter because buyers will know:

- why you want to see them; and
- that you are going to call.

However, whether you write or 'cold call' will be dependent on your company, it's products/services, your target market and your own attitude. Cold calling has the advantage of being quicker. Whichever option you decide upon, you will need to project yourself well and be in a positive frame of mind.

Timing of your call

The timing of your call can determine whether or not you will get an appointment. You won't be aware of what buyers are doing at the time of your call. When you get to speak to them it is polite to ask if it is convenient to talk. If they say yes, you have their attention and can proceed. If they say no, (or are too busy to talk to you now) try to commit them to a time when it is convenient for them to talk to you.

There are disadvantages in doing this, for example, they might:

- not be available when you next call;
- avoid future interaction with you; or
- forget.

If this happens you will need to decide which is the best approach for you. There is no right and wrong; if one doesn't work, try another! Being yourself on the telephone will help you sound natural and convincing.

Your voice

Another factor to consider on the telephone is your voice. You need to:

- Speak clearly
- Pace yourself
- Be relaxed
- Be assertive/sincere
- Be confident
- Smile – be happy, (but not over enthusiastic or too familiar)!

The first impression you give a buyer can mean the difference between getting an appointment and not getting one!

Being formal or informal

If you are contacting someone for the first time it is a good idea to address buyers formally, unless you are invited to talk to them on first name terms. However, you will need to decide how to approach this depending on your market, contact level etc.

Structuring your call

If you have written a letter of introduction you can refer buyers to it when you speak to them. If you decide to do a cold call, you will need a reason or 'introduction benefit'. The stronger this is, the more impact your call will have. In this section we will focus on cold calling on the telephone.

Your 'introduction benefit' should include a strong **hook** and **benefit** to the person you are speaking to. You should state why you want to see him/her. It should be shorter than an introductory letter. On the telephone, people have less of an attention span compared with reading something or having a face-to-face meeting.

You can use some of the material from an introductory letter to achieve this.

Example 1

Introduction to Mr T Ronson – Production Director of a packaging company.

Hello, Mr Ronson? (*Yes*),

Is it convenient to talk to you? (*Yes*)

I'm John Simmons from Inventory Management Limited.

Hook: As the head of production I'm sure you'll be looking for new ways to maintain production levels and get extra value for money from a supplier.

Benefit: We have helped companies achieve this. I would like to make an appointment to see you to establish how we can help.

Close

Example 2

Introduction to Mrs S Partoni – IT Manager of an Insurance company.

> Hello, Mrs Partoni? (Yes), I'm Jane Byford from ABC Software Limited
>
> **Hook:** Many of our customers are looking for new ways to maximise the 'uptime' of their network capability
>
> **Co. Benefit:** I would like to make an appointment to see you to discuss how we have helped companies prevent loss of information in the event of a network breakdown.
>
> **Close**

PRACTICAL POINTER

When you are presenting your introduction benefit, be careful not to offer financial savings as the only/main incentive.

If you do, you will then be under pressure to deliver savings. This is at a time when you don't know enough about the target account to necessarily be able to achieve this. Also, this type of incentive may set the wrong tone for your first meeting. How do you know if you can save a buyer money? You would be better advised to talk about *value for money* solutions.

Unless your role is to sell on the telephone, don't get into a long conversation about your company and it's products. Even if a buyer wants to talk about them, you can do this at your first appointment! The next step, once you have asked for an appointment is what to do if a buyer does not see a benefit in seeing you!

Overcoming objections on the telephone

Objection prevention is better than having to overcome an objection at all! However, it is common for a buyer to resist a request for a meeting. Many buyers are professionally trained in dealing with salespeople and don't want to spend time continually looking for additional supplier's!

PRACTICAL POINTER

To overcome an objection on the telephone, focus on the appointment rather than the objection itself. By doing this you will avoid in getting into 'specifics' and concentrate on the solution – a face-to-face meeting.

If you do get an objection from someone, try the following template to overcome it and gain an appointment:

Structure =

Pause – Empathise – Benefit – Close

Pause

This allows you time to think of an appropriate response as well as let buyers know that you have listened to them.

Empathise

To show empathy, consider starting your sentence with "I understand/I appreciate". This will show buyers that you respect their concern.

Benefit

Give the reason why you still think that there is a benefit in a buyer seeing you.

Close

Focus on times and dates!

Common telephone objections

I'm not interested

Pause: I appreciate that you may not be interested in something that you haven't seen, but I would still like the opportunity to explain to you how we have helped other companies like yours **+ close.**

Tell me about it now

Pause: I can talk to you about it now but it would be better if I could talk to you about the benefits in person **+ close.**

I'm too busy

Pause: I respect that you must be busy. That is the reason I am calling, to make an appointment to meet with you in person at a mutually convenient time **+ close.**

I don't deal with this

A = If not the right person – **pause** – Please could you tell me who does?

B = If it is the right person – **pause** – I appreciate that you might not get involved in all aspects of this. However, I would like to meet you to discuss the benefits as you are an important part of the decision-making process **+ close.**

Send me literature

Pause: I can send you literature. However, in order to get a better understanding of how we might help you I would like to make an appointment to meet you + **close.**

You're wasting my time

Pause: I respect that your time is valuable. However, I wouldn't consider it a waste of your time if I could pass on the benefits that other companies have gained through working in partnership with us + **examples** + **close.**

I already have a supplier, (enough suppliers)

Pause: I understand that you already use another supplier, (other suppliers), however there have been a number of developments that I feel might benefit you + **examples** + **close.**

You are too expensive

Pause: I appreciate that you would only be looking to discuss benefits that would bring you value for money. We would never introduce a solution to a company which wasn't cost-effective to you + **close.**

I have had a bad experience

Pause: I'm sorry to hear that you've had a bad experience with us/a similar product/service, but there have been a number of new/exciting developments. I would like to discuss this issue with you in person + **close.**

Empathy means that you appreciate the buyer's point of view. You do not have to commit yourself as to whether you actually agree with it! This will help you maintain a balanced, calm approach which will relax a buyer, to gain the commitment you need for a first appointment.

You also need to be assertive, (not aggressive), so that you maintain control of the conversation. **If buyers control the conversation then you lessen the chance of gaining an appointment.** This is because they will have longer to talk themselves out of seeing you. Another pitfall to avoid is taking questions about your company and its products and services. This could give a buyer another reason not to see you.

Some questions can be buying signals but you don't have the knowledge of their situation to know this. That is why it is best to answer as little as you feel you need to before stating your preference to discuss it at an appointment. Telephoning a buyer for the first time can be challenging. But it is much easier if you are prepared and have a structure in place to help you.

The next step is to have an agenda for your first appointment and to begin a dialogue with something that is interesting and differentiates you from your competitors!

Key questions

When you meet buyers for the first time it is new for both parties – you don't know them and they don't know you. This is why you should start off with a partnership approach, to help build confidence in you and your company. This can be hard to communicate because you have to earn credibility. To do this you need to be professional, build a rapport and ask relevant questions.

The way you create a relevant agenda is to revert back to your call-objectives (as discussed in Chapter 2 – Targeting new accounts, (*Recording sales call information*). Once you have introduced yourself to a new contact and participated in a degree of 'small talk' you should consider leading into your agenda by asking a 'Key Question'.

What is a 'Key Question'?

A key question will link your introduction to your agenda and call objectives. It is designed to start a discussion between a buyer and you about a subject that has strategic value rather than product/service value. It is meant to be an 'icebreaker' or introduction issue to involve a buyer.

If delivered well, a 'Key Question' will help buyers to relax. This should make it easier to develop the sales call well.

Examples of key questions

- How is the current level of sales in your market affecting your production levels?
- What effect is the competition having on your business?
- How do you think the growth of the Internet is going to affect you?

- What key issues are currently top of your company's agenda?
- Where do you see your own company's growth coming from over the next five years?

By asking one or two questions like this (personalised to your buyer's market) you increase the chances of creating a good impression. Other factors you need to consider are the buyer's:

- job role;
- level of experience; and
- use of your type of product/service.

Let us look at a typical first appointment structure to see where a 'Key Question' would be asked:

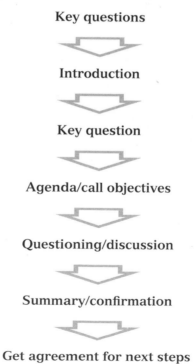

Key questions

Introduction

Key question

Agenda/call objectives

Questioning/discussion

Summary/confirmation

Get agreement for next steps

When should a key question be used?

A 'Key Question' should be:

- used as an introduction to support your call objectives.

- concise and relevant.

- written down before you go in.

- about something which is relevant to the person you are seeing.

- To do with the 'overall picture' of either the target company or the industry.

There are two other important distinctions to make about a 'Key Question':

1 it is **not** generally product related; and

2 it is an **open** question (i.e. it begins with how, why, what, who or where)!

This gives buyers an opportunity to answer the question in detail. This will encourage them to talk more openly.

A 'Key Question' can help to differentiate you from a competitor. It can strengthen a buyer's perception of you as a potential business partner because you are showing interest in their job role and company. It gives you an opportunity to understand their views on a relevant subject and how their role fits in with this. It also links very well into your main call objectives as the next part of your sales call.

Chapter summary

In this chapter we have looked at:

- Introductory telephone techniques.

- Cold calling on the telephone.

- Overcoming objections on the telephone.

- Key questions.

Introducing yourself to a target account normally requires using the telephone. This can be helped by being prepared, having a good structure and with practice! By taking the time to do this you will improve your chances of getting a first appointment and create a good impression. Telephoning a buyer for the first time will involve having a good introduction technique and being able to handle common objections in a confident manner.

Asking a 'Key Question' can help you to make a good first impression. It can also make it easier for buyers to trust and respect you.

Key points

✓ Do some preparation before you make a new business telephone call.

✓ Focus on the benefit your new contact will get from a meeting.

✓ Don't go into 'specifics' about your product/service.

✓ Be assertive and confident and be ready to overcome objections.

✓ When opening a call, ask a key question – this will help create a good impression.

Coaching table

1. Decision-maker met?	2. Status	3. Self-development points
Has the decision-maker confirmed spend?	Decision-maker not identified/met	Identify and meet decision-maker
	Met decision-maker and budget should be available this month	Ensure that buying process is understood and decision-maker has confirmed spend
	Met decision-maker/budget holder. Budget confirmed for this month	Meet other key players involved in buying decision and gain commitment

CHAPTER **FOUR**

Turning interest into commitment

Turning interest into commitment

Introduction

Asking a 'Key Question' is a good link to the next part of developing a sale. That is, to begin asking buyers general questions about their business. We are now going to look at how to get commitment from buyers by having good questioning (and listening) skills.

By the end of this chapter you will be able to:

- Choose the right balance between open/closed questions and talking/listening.

- Ensure that buyers have a genuine need for your product/service.

- Get buyers to want to buy from you.

- Turn interest into commitment!

This will enable you to develop a sale properly and improve your chances of turning a prospect into a customer. If you are one of several suppliers, it will help you to win a larger share of the more profitable business available. Although we will use a first appointment as our example, the information in this chapter is often applied over a number of meetings. How you apply these skills will depend on the product/services you sell and the market you are in.

Questioning and listening

A time when many salespeople know that something has gone wrong in the sales process is when it's too late – and an order is lost! A common reason given for this happening is that a person's closing techniques were not good enough. This may be true, but it is also common to find that his/her questioning and listening skills contributed to this.

If this happens, it can be because you haven't got the genuine commitment you need in order to close a sale. This can result in price-driven buying decisions and a higher proportion of lost sales! By asking good questions you will move through the stages of a sale at the right time and with the right level of commitment before closing.

Solution selling

In order to differentiate yourself and your company from others, follow a process of good questioning techniques. This will help buyers to realise that they have a genuine need which your company is in the best position to meet.

Competition has increased in many markets in the past ten years. Customers have found that no single supplier has an edge and if one does it doesn't last for long. Suppliers have had to look at different ways to gain a competitive advantage.

Suppliers often have to look at different ways to gain a competitive advantage. Looking at the type of relationship customers want and matching your products and services to it can achieve this.

By exceeding a customer's expectations you are more likely to win business in the first place and maintain it. This is what 'Solution Selling' is all about, looking for a particular issue of concern to a customer and gaining genuine commitment to your solution to it.

We will now look at beginning a discussion with a target buyer. The type of questions you ask buyers will depend on their:

- Level of responsibility – (Senior, Middle management or Influencer level).

- Role – is he/she the decision-maker?

- Company structure and buying policy.

- Attitude towards your company (and their own).

- Relationship with your competitors.

- Personality, experience and market knowledge.

- The relationship they have with other key players involved in the buying process.

- Level of training.

Before you start to ask questions about the buyer's requirement you should go through your agenda. Ask a buyer if they would like to include something. Check with a buyer that it is all right for you to ask questions and make notes. This is polite and will help you and him/her to relax. You should establish how long the buyer has for the meeting. Most appointments don't usually last more than an hour.

It is *not* advisable to make notes on a laptop (personal computer) as this can act as a barrier to a buyer. We can now look at the structure of an appointment:

Questioning techniques

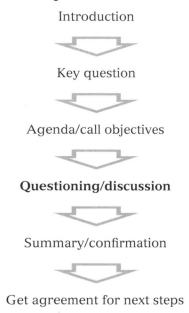

Introduction

Key question

Agenda/call objectives

Questioning/discussion

Summary/confirmation

Get agreement for next steps

Ask questions to gain a better understanding of a target account's buying and decision-making process.

Open questions

At this stage, up to eighty per cent of your questions should be open ones, beginning with, '*What – Who – How – Why – When – Where – Which*'. By using them you are more likely to get a buyer to talk.

Closed questions look for a yes/no answer and are likely to begin with *'Would – Will – Could – Can – Do – Does – Did – Have – Has – Is – Are'*. They should be used to:

1 Check your understanding of something.

2 Summarise a particular situation.

3 Close for the next steps.

Think about the type of questions you ask and the balance between open and closed ones. This will help you to get the right information you need to develop the sale well.

Too many open questions can lead to a buyer becoming bored. It can also lead you to have information about your target account that might not be relevant to a sale.

Not enough open questions can mean that you won't have enough information to develop the sale properly. You might then be tempted to close too early. If this happens you are more likely to receive objections because buyers will not have committed themselves to valuing your solution highly enough.

Too many closed questions can lead buyers to think that you are controlling the conversation. It can also mean that you don't let them go into the level of detail they would like to in order to explain aspects of their situation. This could also lead to a buyer becoming agitated or frustrated with you.

Not enough closed questions can lead to a lack of commitment and no obvious need for any next steps. If you don't ever summarise with a closed question, you might not have the correct understanding about the current situation. If a buyer does not want to develop a sale with you, asking too many closed questions will make it harder to find this out.

One common trait some salespeople have is to start off by asking an open question and then turning it into a closed one! For example: What type of products do you buy, type X I suppose? Try and avoid doing this, as it will reduce the impact of your question and the information you get from a buyer.

Like most sales situations it is about getting the balance right, using your common sense (and experience) to challenge yourself. Ask your sales manager for feedback after discussing this part of the sale with you.

The correct balance between talking and listening

Another factor that will affect your questioning skills is to look at the balance between how much you talk and how much you listen. Ideally you should consider listening for about two thirds of the time. This is to encourage buyers to explain aspects about their buying situation. This will be more difficult if you are doing all the talking!

Salespeople have a natural tendency to want to talk. Those who tend to talk more than a buyer also tend to close too early. They have a tendency to rush and are less likely to develop a sale well. Many people assume that listening is a passive response to someone talking. This can mean that you might not hear what someone actually says or means which can mean that you develop a sale in the wrong way. Most of us think four times quicker that we speak, so really listening to someone is challenging.

Let us now look at barriers to effective listening and possible solutions:

Barriers to good listening

X Focusing on what we think is important (without qualifying this).

X Thinking 'ahead' of what is being said by someone.

X Listening more to something that is of interest to us/ switching off' if it isn't.

X Having preconceived ideas of what someone means.

X Becoming distracted, tired or bored.

X Not liking the person we are listening too (or what he/she says).

Possible solutions

✓ Being more patient with the person you are talking to.

✓ Fully understanding a situation before you respond to it.

✓ Listening to what someone means, as well as what they say.

✓ Remaining objective.

✓ Putting yourself in the buyer's situation.

✓ Relaxing.

✓ Improving the quality, relevance and meaning of the questions you ask.

✓ Trying to concentrate more.

Listening to someone can be tiring and requires patience. Other factors that will affect a buyer's level of participation in a sales call are:

- What you say.

- How you say it.

- How relevant it is.

- Where you put it in the conversation.

- Your knowledge of the account.

- Your relationship with the buyer.

- Your attitude/motivation/enthusiasm.

- Your level of experience.

- The pace you speak at and intonation of your voice.

If this part of the sales cycle is done well, the next steps become easier.

Good questioning techniques are perhaps the most under-valued, overlooked aspect of the entire sales cycle. This could be because they are taken for granted and salespeople don't always appreciate that they hold the key to getting the right information in developing a sale and the business relationship well.

Having a structure

Most buyers won't change suppliers on price alone (although they can give business to one existing supplier at the expense of another because of this). To change suppliers altogether, they normally have some area of dissatisfaction, issue or need that an existing supplier cannot meet in full (or is not performing well in).

Buyers don't have the time or the inclination to keep changing suppliers. Also, many are very experienced in dealing with sales-people and can find it hard to distinguish you from other suppliers. Having a structure to your questioning techniques can help you to manage an appointment well.

Distinguishing yourself

Being structured will help you to distinguish yourself from your competitors. As we mentioned earlier, one of the main D.S.P's (distinguishing selling points) that you should look to develop is your questioning skills.

If you progress a sale in the correct way, you will be able to shape a buyer's thinking. You will be able to focus buyers to re-evaluate why they buy a particular product/service. You can then look at the gaps between what they have and what they would like to have and develop this into a genuine need.

Most buyers consider the sales issues when choosing a supplier – View of your company/your competitors/your products and services etc. Some areas may be more important than others although all buyers will want value for money!

Even if a buyer prefers you to a competitor, he/she will be under pressure to get the best 'deal'. Adopting an 'over-friendly' manner in the hope that you will build a relationship quicker can appear false and will lessen your chances. Also, being on good terms with a buyer, on it's own, will rarely be enough to win a sale.

PRACTICAL POINTER

Be yourself, be relaxed, ask relevant questions, be a good listener, and know your products and services as well as those of your competitors. These are the basic ingredients for being successful in most markets and in distinguishing yourself.

Questioning skills structure

Many salespeople look to provide a solution once they have gained some interest from a buyer. They often fail to expand this interest and turn it into commitment. If this occurs too soon, it can mean that buyers:

- have not seen the benefit of a proposed solution; or

- find it hard to differentiate you from your competitors/their existing supplier!

If this happens then you may find that the main focus is on **price!** This is not a way to maintain good profit margins, so let us look at what is.

By asking good *general* questions you should find out relevant information to develop the call. You will then need to look for any current issues by *probing* a buyer and *expanding* an issue. Then, by getting a buyer to describe the *benefit* of solving it and developing the buyer's needs, he/she should then reveal a desire for a *solution*. You can then link the benefits of your product/ service to this:

Advanced questioning techniques

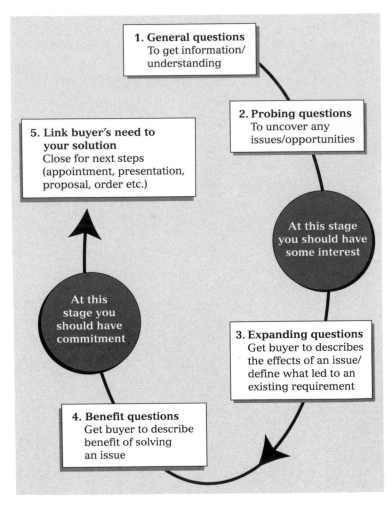

1. **General questions**
   To get information/
   understanding

2. **Probing questions**
   To uncover any
   issues/opportunities

At this stage
you should have
some interest

3. **Expanding questions**
   Get buyer to describes
   the effects of an issue/
   define what led to an
   existing requirement

4. **Benefit questions**
   Get buyer to describe
   benefit of solving
   an issue

At this
stage you
should have
commitment

5. **Link buyer's need to
   your solution**
   Close for next steps
   (appointment, presentation,
   proposal, order etc.)

Asking good relevant questions will make it easier to get the right information and develop the sale. This will involve you being structured. By doing this, buyers will find it easier to understand you and you will increase their involvement in the process. The next step is to look at this template in more detail, with examples of the types of question that you can use to help you.

Advanced questioning techniques

The Huthwaite Research Group have carried out work on the psychology of selling called 'Behaviour Analysis'. Their SPIN® methodology showed that good questioning techniques were a key determinant in developing a sale well and gaining genuine commitment.

We can now look in more detail at what buyers are interested in compared with what they will commit to. We will follow a process that can help you to ensure that you can develop a need that a buyer is prepared to act upon. If you can achieve this it is easier to link a defined need to your solution.

Advanced questioning techniques can be used in new accounts and with existing customers. Our examples focus more on the former. To maximise their impact you will need to:

- Adapt your questioning style to different types of buyer/ account;

- Phrase questions in a way that you (and a buyer) are comfortable with; and

- Use terminology that is relevant to your market.

By having a consultative approach you will also find it easier to involve buyers in the process. We will now look at the five key areas.

1. General questions

These provide basic facts about what is happening now and the buyer's situation. More information is gained by asking open questions (information seeking). These are 'General' questions about the buyer's business/suppliers/current buying situation.

For example:

- What type of equipment do you use?
- How many suppliers do you have?
- What type of transport facilities have you got?
- Who is your network provider?

Once you feel you have enough information about the general situation you need to start probing in areas in which a buyer might have some level of dissatisfaction. This is so that you can find out what gaps there are between what the buyer dislikes and what he/she is prepared to live with. If a buyer has a requirement you will still need to find out what caused him/her to get to this stage.

2. Probing questions

Questioning buyers about any current frustrations that they currently have will help you to identify an issue or understand why an opportunity has arisen. If you are successful in finding out about something that is affecting a buyer (especially with another supplier) you should get interest from them. By itself this will not lead to a sale, it needs to be developed.

Asking 'Probing' questions can do this. They need to be asked in a sensitive way so that a buyer feels relaxed about giving you the right information. For example:

- How do you find your current supplier's service?'

- What do you think of the 'system' you have in place?

- What quality standards does your current supplier offer?

- If there was one area that you could ask your current supplier to improve upon, what would it be?

Another way of asking a 'Probing' question is to make a statement trying to get a buyer to agree with it. If a buyer accepts this, then ask an open question (as above) about it and find out what they find frustrating.

For example:

- Our experience has found that sometimes deliveries can be late; do you find that?

  If 'Yes' – Why are they? If 'No' – Make another statement/ask another question

- Do you have any quality issues?

  If 'Yes' – What are they? If 'No' – Make another statement/ask another question

At this stage you should be looking at what is happening, NOT how the buyer feels). You are looking to probe in the 'sales issues' areas.

PRACTICAL POINTER

If your company is the existing supplier in an account you will need to be more sensitive about how you ask your questions. This will help ensure you don't uncover areas of dissatisfaction that could lead a buyer to want to change suppliers! However, you still want to be aware of any potential issue/opportunity to put yourself in a position to decide how to deal with it.

Don't focus on your products or price at this stage because this:

- Won't distinguish you from your competition.

- Won't make it easy for a buyer to expand an issue.

- Will lead a buyer to focus on a solution.

Now, a buyer should be giving you examples of how an issue occurred and be responsive to your questions.

At this stage you should have developed some interest

This is because you will have discussed areas that buyers are not currently happy with or issues that caused a requirement to exist in the first place. If there are none, then you will still need to probe in the sales issues areas, (view of your company, competitors, you products/services etc). This will help you look for ways to develop other parts of your company's overall offer.

Even if the products you sell are similar to your competitors you should still be able to get buyers to look at other D.S.P's you have. This means that later in the sales cycle, even if your products/services are about the same price, you will have focused on other added value areas that give you an 'edge' over your competitors.

It will be up to you to convince a buyer (through your questioning skills) that these areas do represent value. This is a key point because many companies have several suppliers, all of which might be offering similar (and in some cases the same) products and services.

At this stage, it is unlikely that you will have gained genuine commitment to buy (even if there is a requirement)! This is because the buyer has not seen the value of changing yet (unless you focus on price alone and look to discount). On it's own, your solution, probably won't affect this. You now need to probe for more emotional responses to get buyers to see that a change will genuinely benefit them.

Asking 'Expanding' questions which look for a *negative, emotional response* can help to do this.

3. Expanding questions

It is now the time to ask how a buyer feels about how a particular issue/challenge/difficulty/frustration that is affecting him/her. This can also be applied to new sales opportunities by asking a buyer the 'cost' of not developing a potential requirement. These questions expand an issue and are likely to start with:

- 'How is this affecting...?'

- 'How do you feel about the situation?'

- 'Describe what this means to you?'

This will highlight the importance of an issue and encourage a buyer to want to act and solve it. Typical expanding questions might be:

- How is the delivery issue (which you described as frustrating), affecting you personally + other areas of your business/your company's performance etc?

- How do feel the poor reliability of product X is affecting your customers?

Don't forget to ask how an issue will affect other parts of the buyer's business – his/her immediate manager, other departments, deliveries, morale, supplier relationships etc. Once you have done this two or three times buyers should see for themselves that a gap exists between where they are and where they could be.

Before you consider linking your solution to a buyer's need you will want to bring the buyer's motivation up. If you offer a solution now, he/she will still be frustrated and might blame you for highlighting this! A buyer might not have fully understood the benefit of doing something about an issue/problem/frustration/opportunity. So now is the time to ask 'Benefit' questions to solve this.

4. Benefit questions

'Benefit' questions lift a buyer's motivation and are similar to 'Expanding' questions but they look for a positive emotional response. Don't provide a solution yet and don't discuss your product/service offering at this stage!

Find out how buyers feel and what it would mean to them if an issue was solved or an opportunity was concluded. You can ask how their customers, colleagues, departments, etc would be affected as this will add impact.

This will make buyers feel that they are in control of a situation, which they should now want to solve. For example:

- What would be the benefit to your company if you were to get a more flexible approach?

- If you could solve that issue how would this affect the sales department?

- How would a solution to this make your life easier?

- If you could rely on a supplier to deliver on time how would that improve things?

The better you phrase your questions the more impact they will have.

At this stage you should have developed commitment

Don't be tempted to use benefit questions as a way of closing a sale too early. This is done if you ask a buyer about the benefits of your company solving an issue rather than the buyer solving it. For example, 'if we could solve that issue...' rather than, 'if you could solve that issue...' This will increase the chances of a buyer understanding the benefits of a solution and confirming them to you.

When a buyer has answered two or three benefits questions and is prepared to act on them, it is then time to present your solution.

5. Link buyer's need to your solution

This is the time to close on a particular issue and link your benefits to a buyer's need. For example:

- So, if the product we have does XYZ would you be happy to look at our solution?

- If we could meet your delivery/service requirements better would you consider using us for X, Y or Z products?

- We have a product X that can meet your requirement, would you like to see it?

Remember that this five-stage process could happen in one appointment, or more likely, over several appointments. This will depend on your market, local situation and your target account's buying-cycle. Making this process part of your daily routine will take time, patience and practice. The results will reflect your investment!

Stages 2, 3 and 4 can be easily transferred to a table format that you can take into a call. This will help prompt you to ask the right questions and record the right target account information. For example:

Probing, Expanding and Benefit questions

Probing question	Expanding question	Benefit (of solving issue)
Issue (with current situation)	**Effect it has on the buyer** (His/her dept. and other areas of the company)	**Benefit of the buyer solving it** (His/her dept. and other areas of the company)
Inconsistent/late deliveries	Causes uncertainty and delays in finished product going out	Improve productivity and ability to manage daily routines/ deliveries
Some quality issues	Gives poor image of end product and company	Would stop some product information being returned
Lack of support information	Can't always get up to date information	Would improve marketing support and end-use/ customer relations

Ensure that it is *the buyer* who is confirming the information and not you assuming there is an issue and therefore a need to solve it!

Finally, earn the right to advance from one stage to another. Expect commitment from a buyer at each stage of the sales cycle and be assertive. This will help to maximise the strength of the process and keep a buyer involved.

Good questioning techniques will help you to develop a sale well and gain credibility with a buyer quickly. Developing a way of doing this that suits you will also make it easier to differentiate yourself from other suppliers. It will also make gaining commitment easier from different types of buyer.

Chapter summary

In this chapter we have looked at:

- Questioning and listening.

- Having a structure.

- Advanced questioning techniques.

Developing a sale properly will give you satisfaction and a buyer confidence in you. Focusing on the type of questions you ask and the way in which you ask them can do this. Having good listening skills will ensure that you understand what a buyer says.

Having a structure to work with can help you develop a sales call well. You can also use your questioning skills to gain interest from a buyer by identifying issues. Once you have interest you can then use this to develop commitment and turn the issues into selling opportunities.

Key points

✓ In a sales call, remember to ask good, relevant open questions.

✓ Good questioning and listening skills help to keep a buyer's attention.

✓ Have a structured approach; don't rely on your personality alone!

✓ Be thorough as you move from one questioning stage to another.

✓ Make sure that you have commitment before you offer a buyer a solution.

Coaching table

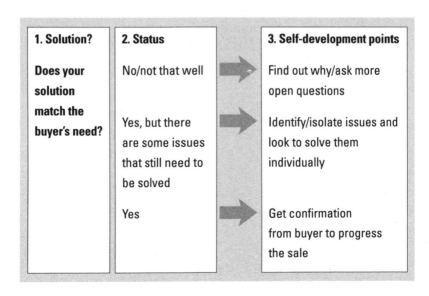

1. Solution?	2. Status	3. Self-development points
Does your solution match the buyer's need?	No/not that well	Find out why/ask more open questions
	Yes, but there are some issues that still need to be solved	Identify/isolate issues and look to solve them individually
	Yes	Get confirmation from buyer to progress the sale

CHAPTER **FIVE**

Developing a sale correctly

Developing a sale correctly

Introduction

In a target account, when you are trying to turn interest into commitment there will be times when you will need to go back in the sales process. This might be because our perception of something needs clarifying or something goes wrong! We will now look at how you can do this to keep a buyer focused on wanting to progress the sale.

Developing a sale properly involves being flexible. If you move from one stage to another properly you improve your chances of gaining genuine commitment.

By the end of this chapter you will be able to:

- Ensure that you have genuine commitment before closing a sale.

- Present solutions to buyers that will benefit to them.

- Overcome any obstacles you might encounter.

- Win more sales by focusing on the buyer's needs.

Ensuring that you have 'genuine' commitment

Many buyers who have a requirement will be looking at more than one supplier. It will not necessarily be in their interest to let you know how committed they are to your solution. This is because a buyer may be weighing up different options with potential suppliers to try and negotiate a better price! You will therefore need to use your selling skills to ensure that you have the right level of commitment before you offer a solution.

Forecasting issues

Checking your perception against reality can begin after a first appointment. Once you have been to one you should look to complete a forecast. This will give you an objective look at your chances of short- and long-term business in the account. It will help you measure the 'gaps' between where you are and where you need to be and act as a 'status' report.

It will enable you to plan a sales strategy in order to win business in the account. As we mentioned in Chapter 2 – Targeting new accounts, (*Forecasting future sales*), you should look at issues like timeframe, product fit, spend etc. This should be updated every time you go into the target account. Dong this will help you to focus on accounts that have the most potential.

You can use a forecasting model to help you assess this. If you do find that you are wasting time on a particular account it is better to see it as early as possible in the sales cycle. By doing this you have more time to alter your strategy.

Buyer consistency

To ensure that you are developing a sale well look for consistency in buyers' answers to your questions and their body language. Note how buyers react to follow-up telephone calls and written correspondence too.

Take into account the pace at which a buyer wants to progress and the internal barriers that he/she faces. If you are unsure about anything, then use your questioning skills to uncover any potential issues that you suspect are there.

'Would Like' versus 'Must Have' needs

Turning interest into commitment is about ensuring that you develop something that a buyer 'Would Like' and would be useful into something they 'Must Have'. This can be defined in the following way:

Defining 'Would Like' and 'Must Have' needs

'Would Like' needs highlight a buyer's issues, attitude and opinions.

THESE ARE LIKELY TO DEVELOP SOME INTEREST

'Must Have' needs highlight a buyer's wants, desires and intentions.

THESE ARE LIKELY TO DEVELOP COMMITMENT

To distinguish between the two, you will want to ensure that you know at what stage you are in your questioning techniques phase (see previous Chapter 4 – Turning interest into commitment, (*Having a structure*), i.e. General, probing, expanding or confirmation questions).

Some of the key points to remember in gaining commitment are:

1   Don't give too much information too early in a sales call, or offer a solution.

2   Uncover and develop a buyer's needs.

3   Check that what you hear is what a buyer has said.

By taking the time to do this (even if it is over a number of sales calls) you are more likely to distinguish between 'Would Like' and 'Must Have needs.

Take the case of a salesperson thinking that he/she has the right level of commitment to offer a solution.

• In Example 1 the salesperson only has interest.

• In Example 2, he/she has genuine commitment.

A likely outcome can be illustrated like this:

The wrong path and the right path!

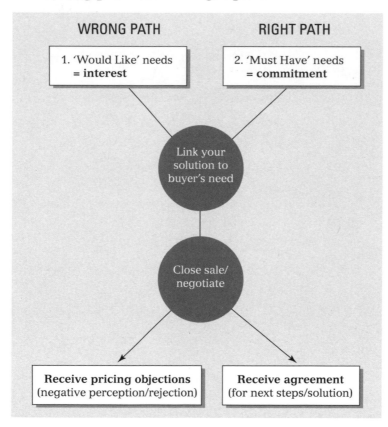

Don't be concerned about going back in the sales cycle when you are not sure if you have genuine commitment. It is advantageous to check that your perception is correct. As we will discuss in Chapter 9 – Closing the sale, objection prevention is better than looking to overcome unnecessary objections from a buyer!

Another way of illustrating that you have the right level of commitment is to draw a line halfway across a blank piece of paper. Look at 'Interest' as above the line and 'Commitment' as below the line. Then compare the two areas and challenge yourself on each one. For example:

Interest or Commitment?

You get interest from understanding:

- General target account information
- Areas of buyer dissatisfaction/issues
- The effects of any area of dissatisfaction
- Why this has arisen
- The reason's behind a buyer's requirement

These create 'Would Like' needs

You get commitment by:

- Getting a buyer to want to act on an area of dissatisfaction/issue
- Discussing an issue and asking expanding and confirmation questions
- Discussing the effects of a buyer not progressing a requirement
- A buyer agreeing that your solution (best) fits his/her need
- Linking your solution to the benefit the target account will get

These create 'Must Have' needs

By creating a table like this you will be able to have an objective look at how much commitment you really have. This will allow you to work on any gaps between what you have and what you need. If this takes one meeting or several, the principle is the same.

In order to focus on getting genuine commitment before linking your solution to a buyer's need, complete this exercise.

'Would Like' versus 'Must Have' needs exercise

Statement	'Would Like' = Interest	'Must Have' = Commitment	
Question		**True**	**False**
1 If you want to persuade, it is better to give information than to seek it			
2 When a buyer shows interest, it is best to offer them an immediate solution			
3 Buyers often buy on price if you haven't received genuine commitment from them			
4 A 'Would Like' need leads to a natural desire of a target account to buy something			

5 One of the best ways of getting commitment from buyers is to get them to raise objections (so that you can overcome them)		
6 My current deliveries are too slow		
7 I'm looking for a reduction in your price		
8 I want to rationalise my spend		
9 I'm not satisfied with one of my current suppliers		
10 I'm interested in that		
11 I'm getting frustrated with their service		
12 If you can do that we can progress		

Answers:

1 **False**: It is better to seek information to gain understanding

2 **False**: This will increase the chances of a buyer raising an objection

3 **True**: They won't see the value of your solution

4 **False**: Not on it's own, it has to be turned into a 'Must Have' need

5 **False**: This will lead to a buyer becoming frustrated

6 **Interest**: This is an opinion, not a statement of intent from a buyer

7 **Commitment**: This is a statement of intent

8 **Commitment**: This is a statement of intent

9 **Interest**: This is an opinion, not a statement of intent from a buyer

10 **Interest**: This is interest, it needs another question to develop it further

11 **Interest**: This is interest, it needs another question to develop it further

12 **Commitment**: This is a statement of intent

If you are not sure about whether the above statements showed signs of interest or commitment ask yourself the following question: Will a buyer act upon this, yes or no?

✓ If the answer is yes, then it is a 'Must Have' need = Genuine commitment.

✗ If not, (or you are not sure), then it is a 'Would Like' need = Interest (and will need further development before offering a solution)

Look at the context of the situation and at how buyers convey a statement to you, their manner, level of conviction and authority. These are all signs as to how committed they are. The next stage, once you have genuine commitment is to link the benefits of your product/service to a solution.

Presenting the benefits of your solution

Gaining commitment is about persuading buyers to want to solve an issue or progress a requirement and to use your company to help them do this.

Offering a solution

When offering a solution you need to ensure that your product/service benefits the target account as well as you! You will also need to present it to the right people. This can involve other key players at different managerial levels as well the buyer. You will need to consider whether or not your contact is the decision-maker!

When you are presenting the benefits of your company remember not only to talk about:

- components/features of your products/service; or

- what they do and how they work.

You *must* link these to how a buyer/target account will benefit. On it's own, information about what a product/service has limited impact. Most people become bored listening to this, so always link your solution to a buyer's need.

If you are relying on a buyer to link a need to your solution and they don't, then either a limited benefit or none at all exists. If you feel this has happened you should go back in the questioning cycle to establish why.

Benefits

The more you describe what your products do, without linking this to a benefit to the buyer, the less impact it will have. If this happens you minimise the chances of that person wanting to progress the sale. Also, it's no good to anyone if you assume that the buyer must have a need. Your assumption could be wrong and the benefit will have little or no impact!

If a buyer is interested in your solution without being committed, he/she might focus on the price of the product rather than its value. This will limit your profit potential. Another factor to consider is that a salesperson who focuses on product features is less likely to succeed than someone who is less friendly but has a good questioning skills.

Benefits are the most powerful way to present your company/ product/service.

Causes of not gaining genuine commitment

Failure to gain commitment can come from a number of key areas other than poor questioning techniques, for example – lack of buyer motivation/budget. If you do get objections after you feel you have commitment from a buyer, consider the following possible reasons:

1. FAILING TO UNDERSTAND THE BUYER'S SITUATION

If you ask few open questions, you may not have enough information from buyers to get genuine commitment. Therefore, ensure that you fully understand their situation and have uncovered real problems they would like to solve or opportunities they would like to develop.

2. TRYING TO GET TOO MUCH INFORMATION

If you try to get too much information by asking too many open questions, buyers can lose interest and become bored. Practice until you are comfortable that you get the right amount of information to progress onto the next stage, and get the buyer's agreement on this.

3. FAILURE TO UNCOVER A PARTICULAR ISSUE

Issues, problems and opportunities are often the main driving forces that stimulate buyers' needs (as well as a new requirement). This is why you must try and uncover 'all' the relevant sales issues. Sometimes a buyer will help you; sometimes he/she might not. You will therefore need to understand a target account's key players, their existing supplier's relationship and product offerings in order to uncover these issues.

4. FAILURE TO GET GENUINE COMMITMENT

As was mentioned earlier, offering a solution without the right level of commitment can lead to a focus on price. If this happens to you regularly, ask yourself if you have established interest and have then looked to offer a solution. You may need to

Look again at your questioning techniques to ensure that you are developing the sale correctly.

5. LOOKING AT THE TYPE OF BUYER/COMPANY YOU ARE SELLING TO

Remember the type of account you are looking to sell into. Skilled salespeople will still find it difficult to win business if a buyer:

- Has very good relationship with another supplier.

- Is not really the decision-maker.

- Buys mainly on price.

- Is not interested in looking at your company as a supplier.

- Has no/little time to discuss the sales issues.

- Is inflexible and rigid in his/her views.

Some buyers will not always want to tell you about an issue or might not want you to help them solve it. If they are happy with their existing supplier then why change? The type of relationship you are able to develop will help you determine how much time to spend on the account.

6. FAILURE TO ASK ENOUGH 'EXPANDING' QUESTIONS

One of the most common challenges salespeople face is that they fail to focus a buyer on the implications of an issue, or understand the motivation behind an opportunity. This is caused by not asking enough/any 'Expanding' questions.

Let buyers describe the effects of the issue or what effect not developing an existing requirement will have. By probing in this area you will help them to *want* to solve the issue. Empathy with their situation will give you a better chance of becoming part of the solution.

7. BUYERS NOT UNDERSTANDING YOUR BENEFITS

If your benefits are weak or not understood they will have little or no impact. *A benefit is only a benefit if buyers can see it for themselves and link it to a need for your product or service!* Make your benefits easy to understand and focus on how they help the target account.

8. FOCUSING ON AREAS IN WHICH YOUR COMPANY IS WEAK

When you ask probing questions, don't focus too much on areas where your company has little or no strengths. By being aware of this you are more likely to develop needs that maximise your chances of providing an acceptable solution.

The timing of presenting your solution and your relationship with a buyer is often the key to winning a sale. However, there are other factors that can influence whether a target account buys from you.

Other sales development factors

One interesting aspect of selling is that every target account has certain differences. You can try a particular line of questioning with one buyer and it works. You try the same line of questioning with a different buyer and it doesn't! Therefore, be prepared to be flexible and treat buyers as individuals.

Cover each issue/opportunity separately

If you get more than one issue or requirement, deal with each one separately (in stages one to five of the questioning skills process, mentioned in the last chapter). You can then get commitment for each one. This will ensure that your questioning techniques are easy to follow.

Try and meet the 'Decision-Maker'

Establish whether your main contact is the decision-maker. In most accounts there are a number of people who 'influence' a sale. But normally, one key person, with authority to spend money is driving the decision-making process. This person may not actually sign an order, he/she might report to someone who does (and who would normally be a director/senior manager). However, a decision-maker will probably be a budget-holder.

A questioning-skills process will have only a limited effect if you use it on someone with little or no authority in the buying process. You can use it to uncover areas of dissatisfaction and develop needs, but you should try to meet the decision-maker as well as people who influence a sale. This will improve your chances of getting genuine commitment.

Develop good interpersonal skills

Consider your own interpersonal skills and questioning style. If you are a submissive person you will need to adapt your style and be more assertive. If you are too assertive, you could put some buyers off. Having good interpersonal skills will involve good manners, listening and being sensitive to a buyer's needs. This will include what you say and how you say it!

This is common sense but your level of ability to adapt in this area will affect how well you interact with people.

Types of sales appointment and market

There are different types of sales appointments – Introduction, second, third, closing appointments as well as account management appointments. Therefore you will need to consider:

- The different type of appointments you make.

- Whether you are in a fast/slow moving market.

- The size and value of your products.

- Your sales cycle.

- A target account's buying cycle.

- The types of people you have met (and need to meet) in a target account.

These issues will affect how easy it is to move from one stage of the sale to another and how long each stage will take.

Timing

You should look at the time you spend on an appointment. If you need to go into more detail about a particular issue or the buyer is under time pressure arrange another appointment. You can then continue from where you left off on the previous one.

Try not to waste time with buyers who could be using you to get better prices from a competitor! This is frustrating and won't achieve the results you want. Focus on accounts where you feel you can add value. By doing this you will be more effective.

A buyer's fixed views

If you feel that a buyer is not helping you, consider whether:

- he/she is objective.

- he/she has a relationship with a competitor that is too 'entrenched' for you to change.

- you are talking to the right person – can you involve other people in the management structure.

- you should change your approach.

Trying to look at a situation objectively will help you to solve many issues on your own. These guidelines will help you to eliminate many mistakes and focus your efforts in the right way. You won't be able to sell to every target account, but you can maximise on the opportunities you do get.

Chapter summary

In this chapter we have looked at:

- Ensuring that you have 'genuine' commitment.

- Presenting the benefits of your solution.

- Other sales development factors.

When you develop a sale well it is easier to get commitment from buyers. Ensuring that you have achieved this is a key requirement in closing a sale successfully. When you present the benefits of your solution make sure that you link them to a target account's 'Must Have' needs. This will increase your chances of buyers wanting to do business with your company.

If you do find that you haven't got the right amount of commitment needed to do this or something has gone wrong, look at possible reasons why. You will need to be objective to achieve this but it will help you isolate the reason so that you can work out the best way to solve it.

Key points

✓ Don't offer a solution once you have gained interest – get commitment first!

✓ Don't confuse 'Would Like' with 'Must Have' needs.

✓ Link what your product/service does to the benefit a buyer will get from it.

✓ If you fail to gain commitment, go back in the sales cycle to establish why.

Coaching table

1. Commitment?	2. Status		3. Self-development points
Do you have the right level of commitment to offer the right solution?	No	→	Look at why and who you are dealing with in the sales process
	Some, but I need more before offering a solution	→	Establish how to get this and look to involve other key players
	Yes	→	Get commitment/ present your offer and look to close

CHAPTER **SIX**

The presentation

The presentation

When you have commitment from a target account you will want to demonstrate how well their needs can be met. Doing an in-depth presentation/ demonstration of your products and services can achieve this.

At the end of this chapter you will be able to:

- Focus on the timing of doing a presentation.

- Be aware of the type of information to include.

- Know when to do a formal and informal presentation.

- Know how to present yourself well.

A good presentation can impress a target account and convince key players in it that your company is the right one to do business with. In order to achieve this you will need to keep it simple and link it to a target account's need.

Let us look at the difference between presentations and demonstrations and the timing of doing both.

Presentations and demonstrations

Presentations (and to a lesser extent demonstrations) are used for two main purposes:

- to link a target account's needs to your solution; and

- as an overview of your products/services and company.

In order to understand when and why you would do a presentation or demonstration, we will define both and look at the timing of when each is normally done.

A **presentation** focuses on explaining about your products/services/company.

A **demonstration** focuses on showing how a product actually works.

Both can be done in front of one person, or several people. Let us now look at using either format as a way of introduction. We can then compare this to when you have a genuine requirement and commitment from a target account.

A presentation/demonstration as an introduction/overview

A presentation or demonstration can be a good way to introduce yourself and your company into a new account. In this context, you are more likely to be general in what you present because you will not know the target account's needs in detail. You will, therefore, have to be careful about assuming what these are. Otherwise you will make assumptions which could turn out to be incorrect.

For this reason you should use a presentation/demonstration at the beginning of a new business relationship as an opportunity to let a target account know that you:

- Understand some of the market issues that are currently affecting (and will affect them in the future).

- Know about their products and services (this can be done by accessing their web site on the Internet).

- Have a history of helping other companies in this market.

- Are keen to begin a dialogue to understand their needs.

Use this type of presentation to get an appointment with the decision-maker as a next step. You don't want to give out too much information about your company and its products (or offer a solution), as this will lessen the need for a face-to-face visit.

Linking a presentation/demonstration to your solution

If a target account has a defined need that you have identified, a buyer will want to know about your solution. A presentation/demonstration is widely used as a 'proof statement' to bring key players in the account together. For many target accounts this is the point where a final decision is made about which company best fits their needs.

If you do this, you will need to:

- separate the 'Must Have' from the 'Would Like' needs;

- present the benefits of both (with more focus on the former); and

- link them to your solution.

This is often the best opportunity you will have to illustrate how your company is in the best position to supply to the target account. It is a logical step to follow before the negotiation process begins and a good opportunity to highlight the value of your solution. By doing this you should find that a buyer is less likely to focus on price!

Timing of your presentation/demonstration

The timing of a presentation/demonstration is a critical factor in how much impact it is likely to have. You will need to decide whether you are presenting as an introduction, before or after you have written a quote or proposal.

There is no definitive rule on the timing but it can be better to present your products and services before you write a proposal. By doing this you can focus on how your product/service meets the target account's needs. By doing a proposal first, you might find that another requirement comes out after your presentation. If this happens you could find that:

- You have to rewrite a proposal.

- A buyer looks to include an additional feature of your product but doesn't want to pay any more for it!

By doing a presentation/demonstration before a proposal you are also more likely to focus the target account on negotiation as the next step. This can encourage buyers to want to negotiate too soon. It may be better to give a buyer a quotation early in a sale and then a more formal proposal once the needs are developed and a budget agreed. This will depend on your market and the target account's buying cycle.

It is not wrong to do a proposal before a presentation; by doing so you encourage a detailed pricing discussion *before* the target account has fully accepted your solution.

Keep the buyer's focus on his/her requirement rather than the cost of your product/service. Link the benefits of your solution to the target account's need in the way that was looked at in Chapter 5 – Developing a sale correctly (*Presenting the benefits of your solution*). By doing this you will maximise the value of your products/services in the buyer's mind. You will also receive fewer objections when you link this to your price because your focus has been on meeting the needs of the target account.

The content, timing and delivery of a presentation/demonstration are important. A poor one (even as an introduction) can lessen your chances of a sale. A good presentation/demonstration can improve your chances of gaining the commitment before you look to negotiate and close the sale. This is why the preparation of a presentation is so important.

What you deliver has to be well-structured and tailored to the target account. The starting point is to look at how to construct a presentation that will meet these introductory or defined requirements.

Preparing presentation material

For the rest of this chapter we will focus on how to present your company and it's products/services to a group of people in the target account. Many salespeople are nervous of doing a 'formal' presentation involving PowerPoint slides. It can be awkward to present to a number of people, some of whom you may not have met before. A good presentation helps to differentiate your company from a competitor.

Preparing slides

Before preparing slides, consider talking for up to thirty minutes with another ten minutes of questions. Any longer in both areas could reduce your impact.

The first step is to decide why you are doing a presentation:

- What is its purpose?
- What is it going to achieve?
- What direction will you take?
- Why should an audience listen to it?
- How do you maintain their interest/keep them involved?

The key to this is to have purpose, give benefits and keep your audience interested. When you are preparing slides there are some guidelines that can help you maximize the effect of your presentation.

Here are ten slide preparation guidelines that you can apply:

Preparing PowerPoint slides

1 Have a title at the top of each slide to identify the content below.

2 Keep your slides simple/easy to read and relevant.

3 Don't have too many lines of text on each slide (up to six).

4 Don't put 'jargon'/unnecessary information in a slide.

5 Don't use a timer in the slide transition to move to the next slide – you might not be ready!

6 Use bullet points, numbers and letters to separate your lines.

7 Be careful about your choice of colour – use sensible colours.

8 Use a 'strap' line at the bottom of a page – to summarise – it adds impact.

9 Don't put too much information in a slide – one line per point!

10 Use UPPER case sparingly – for titles/headings if you feel you have to.

Remember, the purpose of showing slides is to enable your audience to refer to the points *you* are presenting. Therefore, don't read every point word for word – the audience are capable of doing that! Don't forget:

YOU are delivering the message – supported by your visual material!

You will add impact if you know your subject and then focus on the DELIVERY of the presentation.

When you are preparing your slides think about what message you want to give and how you are going to build up a picture in the audience's mind. Ideally, you should consider doing a maximum of up to ten slides. This should be enough to get your message across. More than this number can be too many for an audience to remain interested.

It looks professional to scan in your target account's logo as well as your own (providing the account is happy with this). This gives a 'partnership' feel to the presentation material.

Let us now look at how to build up a simple template in a typical slide.

Slide 1: Looks at providing bullet points in the above format

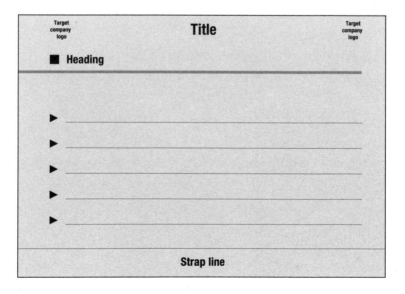

Slide 2: Shows how this might look with information in it.

Target company logo	**Measuring your sales activity**	Target company logo

■ **Forecasting**

▶ Attitude to a partnership approach

▶ Budget for your products and prices you charge

▶ Quality of service they get from you/competition

▶ Timescale to buy from suppliers

▶ Suitability of your products/service

Adding value to your sales focus

Alternative types of slide

You can also use slides to illustrate graphs, pie charts, photos and other information. If you do, keep it simple and easy to understand. If your slides look complicated, so will your products and services! By avoiding this you will make it easier to 'get your message across'.

You can add other visual support material such as photographs.

Slide 3: Uses business photos to support the information.

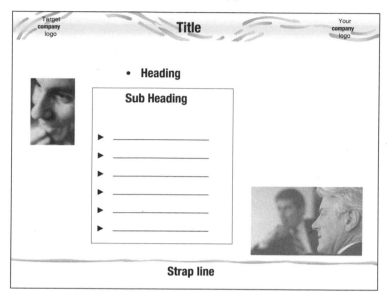

Slide 4: Looks at linking information in a simple way.

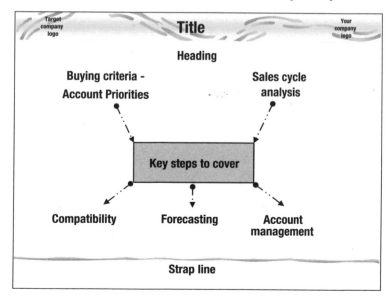

If you are looking to illustrate more 'in-depth' information on a slide, consider 'breaking the information down'. Otherwise your products, services or solution can look complicated or confused. Also, consider the design of the template to ensure that it fits in with the information in the slide.

Slide 5: Illustrates the lack of impact that could be caused by too much information and the choice of design.

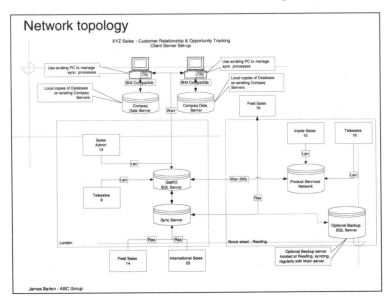

This slide shows how difficult it can be to illustrate more complex information. Some of the limitations include:

- Too much information on one slide.

- Limited choice of background design.

- Difficulty for the audience to understand – reducing impact.

- Difficulty in including logos, titles, headings and strap lines.

- Questions from the audience – which can interrupt your presentation.

You can give handouts to the audience to help. The danger of this is that they then spend time reading this information (and then asking questions) instead of listening to the next part of your presentation. This can be counter-productive, so, **give your handouts at the end**!

In a formal presentation, it is best give these out at the end so that you maintain its flow. By doing this you avoid a 'question and answer' session which you should, ideally, have at the end of your presentation, *not* during it. If you follow this structure you are more likely to remain in control of what you are doing.

Using visual material in the right way will help to maximise the impact of your presentation. The key to this is the thought you put in and this involves good preparation. By keeping your presentation simple and not having too many slides you will make it easier for the audience to understand. This will add more impact.

Let us now look at the actual delivery of the material you prepare.

Informal and formal presentations

When doing a presentation, you will need to consider whether it is to be done informally or formally. In either case you will need to look at how interactive you want it to be. You will also need to decide if you want it discussion-based or you want to take questions at the end of it. These issues highlight a need to plan what you want to achieve.

Informal presentations

An informal presentation tends to have more interaction between the presenter and the audience than a formal one. This has advantages and disadvantages:

ADVANTAGES

The advantage of this is that you can answer questions when they arise and have a good understanding of how well the presentation is going. The atmosphere is also likely to be more convivial.

DISADVANTAGES

The disadvantage is that it can take far longer to complete than a formal presentation. This is because if someone continually interrupts, your pace slows down and this can affect the time it takes to present. This can frustrate other people you are presenting to which may reduce your impact.

The type of presentation you do will depend on what stage of the sales cycle you are at. Remember why you are doing one, to whom, and the message you are looking to get over to your audience. An informal presentation is more likely to be discussion-based and will need less structure than a formal one.

Formal presentations

With a formal presentation you will have to maintain more control. This will make it easier to deliver it in the time you have available.

Let us now look at a structure of a formal presentation:

Eight steps to a good presentation

STEP 1 – INTRODUCTION

- Personal: You, your job title, role, your history in the company

- Company: Brief summary

Ask the audience to keep questions until the end of the presentation. You may cover the point during the session. If not, then they can use the question and answer session at the end to promote a discussion on a particular subject

STEP 2 – INTRODUCTION BENEFIT

- Reason for being there

- Benefit to the audience in listening

STEP 3 – AGENDA

- Let the audience know what the presentation consists of – (i.e. Product X & Y)

- Reasons to do business with your company

- Other information – environmental issues etc

STEP 4 – YOUR PRODUCT/SERVICE OFFERING

Main body of presentation

- Your products/services

- Your understanding of the target account's needs

STEP 5 – REASONS TO DO BUSINESS WITH YOUR COMPANY

- Your distinguishing selling points – D.S.P's

STEP 6 – OTHER ISSUES

- Environment
- IT
- Marketing
- Finance

STEP 7 – SUMMARY

- A short summary on your product offering and company benefits

This should not a repeat of steps 5 and 6 but something like, "If there is one reason why I feel that you should buy Product X/do business with us, it would be..." This is the last piece of information that the audience is likely to remember so the stronger this is the better!

STEP 8 – THANK THE AUDIENCE

- Discuss next steps
- Prepare to answer questions

Handling questions

Remember to inform the audience that there will be time at the end of the presentation for a question and answer session. (as was mentioned in Step 1 – Introduction). This will help your flow and stop you being continually interrupted.

However, during your presentation, if someone genuinely doesn't understand or agree with a part of what you are saying, you may find this difficult to do. This can also be true if the person interrupting you is a director! If it happens you might have to answer an occasional question.

At the end of your presentation you should ask the audience if they have any questions. If someone does ask one, consider what might lie behind it? It could be:

- A need for clarification on something.

- To resolve a doubt.

- A need for more information (about your products/ services/ company).

If no one asks a question, consider asking a rhetorical one and then answering it, e.g. "A question I often get asked is...". If someone asks a stupid question, treat it seriously and don't patronise the person asking it. A persistent question from someone should be taken 'offline' or used as a reason to meet that person to discuss it later or at another time.

If you don't know the answer to a question say you will come back with a complete answer. Providing it is not something that you should know, you can't be expected to understand everything about some product, service or company issues. The commitment you must make is to find out and reassure the person asking it that you will come back to him/her.

You can also ask members of the audience a question to check their level of understanding and commitment. This will depend on the time available, the audience and how well you feel the presentation has gone.

How you deal with a question and answer session will depend on whether you are doing a presentation:

- as an introduction to your company; or

- to link a defined need to your solution.

Whatever type you are doing, use a structure to help you.

Try to tailor your presentation to the type of people who will be listening to it and the situation and look to take control. Thirty minutes can be a long time to talk to a group of people, especially if a large order is depending on it. This means that your professionalism, interpersonal skills and delivery will be as important as the structure and content of the presentation.

You – the presenter

One of the most under-rated parts of a presentation is the focus on you – the presenter. Your ability to convince an audience about your products and services suitability will be a key determinant in it's success. Factors like your positioning, voice, mannerisms and dress sense will all have an impact on this.

Most of all, an audience will be reassured by someone who is knowledgeable and confident. For this to happen you will need to be well-rehearsed and have a good structure to your presentation.

Do's and don'ts of presenting

It is often a small number of things done well that distinguishes one presenter (and company) from another. Let us now look at some of the main points (opposite) to remember when you are delivering a presentation.

DO

✓ Be professional, confident and show enthusiasm.

✓ Try to appear relaxed – enjoy it!

✓ Look smart and wear something that you feel relaxed in.

✓ Speak clearly and at a moderate pace.

✓ Be aware of your body language – be open-minded.

✓ Look interested (and try to be interesting)!

✓ Be clear and concise – keep your message simple.

✓ Use prompts if necessary – (in bullet form so they are easy to read).

✓ Practice on colleagues first.

✓ Have good eye-contact with everyone.

✓ Be aware of the type of people in the audience/their level of experience.

✓ Be aware of the lighting, heating, seating, materials and facilities.

✓ Pause occasionally, it helps both parties to reflect.

✓ Focus on the benefits from your Company, products and services.

✓ Smile, use occasional humour, but keep it light hearted and decent!

✓ Use words and phrases that are likely to add impact.

✓ Use humour if you want but maintain a professional approach.

✓ Stick to a timeframe.

✓ Show a whole slide at a time – it makes it easier to follow.

DON'T

X Keep your hands in your pockets or behind your back.

X Be worried about expressing yourself with your hands.

X Put yourself under pressure.

X Criticise your competitors.

X Walk around the room, try and stay in one place.

X Avoid words like 'uhm' – take your time and think about what you say.

X Look down at your notes too much, it reduces eye contact.

X Rely on PowerPoint slides too much – they should support you!

X Give too much factual information – people don't remember it.

X Hold a pen, it reduces your chance for expression.

X Use words/phrases that an audience is unlikely to understand.

X Rush; you are likely to be nervous – so pace yourself!

X Give out handouts, they distract people – leave them until the end.

X Worry about showing support information to someone in the audience.

X Become too familiar, it will reduce your level of authority.

X Repeat yourself, if you can avoid it!

X Make your slide show too 'flashy'.

Using some of these simple disciplines will make it easier for you to add impact and get your message across. The more you practice before you do a 'live' presentation, the better you will become at presenting.

Communication

Good communication with the audience increases your chances of getting your message across in the right way. This can be done with a good structure and delivery. You can use words and gestures to convey your message as well as visual examples. Poor communication can be caused by:

- Lack of knowledge.

- Weak explanations.

- Poor preparation/delivery.

- Misunderstandings and distractions.

To avoid this happening, remember that an audience has a need for:

- Specific information relating to your key points.

- Involvement.

- Recognition.

This will make them feel part of the presentation and help to maintain their interest and support. A good presentation can lead to an increase in the desire for a target account to trade with you. If you get this part right, the next steps, whether they be at the introduction stage or negotiation and closing stage, become easier.

Remember to outline the key points, summarise your main message and prepare for the next steps. This will be dependent on the type of presentation you do and what stage you are at in the sales cycle.

Being natural and well-prepared are key components in giving a good presentation. It can be a powerful way to convince a group of people to buy from you. Using a structure to support your delivery will increase your chances of it being successful.

Chapter summary

In this chapter we have looked at:

- Presentations and demonstrations.

- Preparing presentation material.

- Informal and formal presentations.

- You – the presenter.

We have also looked at the differences between a presentation and a demonstration. Both involve an ability to adapt to different types of target account and people. Your structure and delivery will affect how well you are received. In a presentation you will need to bear in mind the type of visual effects you show, which will probably include giving a PowerPoint presentation.

You will need to consider whether you are doing a formal or informal presentation. There will be a different focus for each type. Remember, an important part of the process is your ability to persuade a target account of the benefit of doing business with your company. This will involve you being well prepared, relaxed and believing in yourself!

With experience it will become easier and help you to give a good, confident presentation. This will also make it easier for a buyer in a target account to progress a sale with you.

Key points

✓ Look at what a target audience will get from your presentations/demonstration.

✓ Choose the timing and the reasons for doing a presentation carefully.

✓ Use PowerPoint slides/visual material to *support you*!

✓ Have a simple structure and maintain control during your presentation.

✓ Relax, be yourself and enjoy your time presenting.

Coaching table

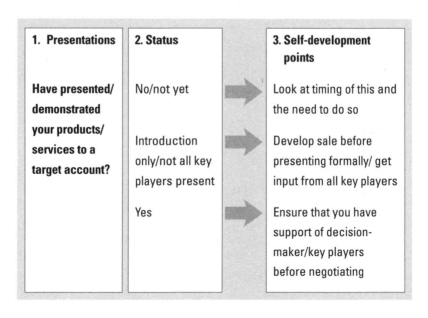

1. Presentations	2. Status	3. Self-development points
Have presented/ demonstrated your products/ services to a target account?	No/not yet	Look at timing of this and the need to do so
	Introduction only/not all key players present	Develop sale before presenting formally/ get input from all key players
	Yes	Ensure that you have support of decision-maker/key players before negotiating

CHAPTER **SEVEN**

The sales proposal

The sales proposal

Introduction

Presenting your solution to a target account will confirm that it can meet their needs. This is a stage that a buyer will often need a more detailed confirmation of the financial investment in your product and service.

At the end of this chapter you will be able to:

* Know what and when to confirm something in writing.

* Link your written confirmation to a target account's need.

* Structure your quotations and proposals to maximise their impact.

* Use them to confirm the buyer's commitment to you.

Many buyers will expect some type of written confirmation of your solution. We will look at the timing for doing this as well as the reasons why this is needed.

Establishing that you are at the proposal stage

Deciding when to put something in writing or in an email will depend on the type of market you are in. It will also depend on the price of your products, the type of relationship you have with a buyer and the length of your sales cycle.

For low-cost, fast-turnover products you might need to send written confirmation after a first meeting. If you sell high-cost products, you will take longer to gain genuine commitment. This means that a detailed proposal will be needed to link your solution to the target account's needs.

PRACTICAL POINTER

Written confirmation, on it's own, is unlikely to turn interest into commitment.

Timing

The timing of any written confirmation can be a key factor in a buyer making a decision in your favour. For high-cost products that have a longer sales cycle, this decision might not happen until *after* a presentation has been done on the product and is likely to include a number of key players, not only the buyer. It is this point, in many cases where target accounts actually make their buying decisions.

Once target accounts have seen your product and have a written pricing confirmation they will often want to move to the negotiation stage. You will therefore, need to manage the presentation and proposal stages well to ensure that you are ready to do the same. If you don't, you could find that you are negotiating without genuine commitment.

Should this happen, the benefits of your solution will have less/ little impact. It is more likely to become something that a buyer uses mainly to compare different suppliers, prices, which you want to avoid.

It may be better to give a buyer an idea of how much your solution will cost early in a sale, as a guide, without going into too much detail. This can be done verbally, by email or in writing confirming that your solution will cost between £X and £Y and it should be brief and linked to a target account's budget. Buyers don't like the idea of committing themselves to a solution too early because they have not:

- Properly surveyed the market.

- Fully confirmed their needs/budget.

- Made a decision about which supplier has the most potential.

Use your common sense, understand your market and have the discipline to hold back from giving too much information too early. You want a good reason to keep developing the sale and the relationship with a buyer. Take your time to get the right level of commitment needed to progress the sale properly.

Other influencing factors

Other factors that will influence the timing of your quote/proposal relating to a target account will include the ten areas mentioned in the forecasting model, Chapter 2 – 'Targeting new accounts', (*Forecasting future sales*). These include – timescale, competition, spend etc.

These areas should be looked at regularly to ensure that they are being developed. You can refer to your forecasting model to do this. You should also consider whether you are writing a quote or a proposal!

Difference between quotations, proposals and tenders

Written confirmation of an offer normally comes in the form of a quotation or a proposal. It is important to establish the difference between the two, what action each performs and what information should be included and excluded. This becomes even more crucial if you are asked to complete a tender!

Importance of written confirmation

It is a good discipline to confirm verbal offers and areas of agreement in writing. This is because:

- A buyer might forget what you discussed.

- He/she might show a quotation/proposal to someone else internally.

- It can help distinguish you from a competitor.

- It focuses a buyer on the benefits of your products/service, not only the price!

Let us now look at the difference between a quotation, proposal and tender.

QUOTATIONS

A quotation is short confirmation of your products/services and your price.

It is more likely to be done earlier in the sales cycle as a brief confirmation of a target account's needs and pricing offer. A quotation should be brief and illustrate benefits in bullet point format only. It will ideally be on one or two sheets of paper, perhaps between 500 – 1,000 words. This might include a price (or price indication) as well as some confirmed needs. Whether these needs are 'Would Like' or 'Must Have' will depend on the type of products you sell and your sales cycle.

PROPOSALS

A proposal is a more detailed confirmation and will have a more detailed link between your prices and a buyer's confirmed 'Must Have' needs.

It would ideally be between two and ten pages in length or between 1,000 – 5,000 words (two to ten A4 pages). It would be presented after a number of meetings and at a point when a target account is closer to making a buying decision. This is because you will be in a better position to know how you are going to link the benefits of your solution at this stage in the sales process!

If you decide to email a quotation or proposal you should consider providing a hard copy by delivering it personally or posting it. A hard copy looks professional and will add more impact if a buyer needs to show it to someone else in the target account.

Whether you post or deliver your quotation/proposal will depend on:

- The price and value of your offer.

- Your relationship with the buyer.

- Timing in the sales cycle.

- The ease of visiting the target account.

You will be more likely to deliver a proposal as it will be more detailed than a quote. It is important that the buyer understands it and agrees with it's contents. It is better to present this in person, especially if the value of your solution is high. It also gives you an opportunity to:

- get a better understanding of a buyer's reaction; and

- discuss any changes that might need to be made if he/she is to present it internally.

If buyers understand and agree with your proposal it will be easier for them to convince other key players in the target account. Any questions or doubts are more easily addressed if you present your offer personally. You should consider whether to send a copy to the finance director/other senior managers involved in the buying process. This would, naturally, need to be done with the approval of the buyer.

Ensuring that you have fully understood the target account's needs and met them is vital. By taking the time to do this you increase the chances of your proposal being fully understood and liked your company being the preferred solution/supplier.

TENDERS

An 'invitation to tender' is a detailed request by an organisation who wants a written response to a large number of well-defined requirements. This can include how a contract would be delivered, (if it was won), as well as an expectation of how the 'customer-supplier' business relationship should be managed.

Your company's response to a tender is also likely to be detailed – possibly in excess of 20 A4 pages or up to 10,000 words. It will cover issues such as:

- Product/service requirements.
- How the target account is to be managed.
- Defined pricing schedules.

It can be used as a basis for a legally binding contract between a target account and supplier and is likely to be formal and direct in its tone. It can include pre-defined questions or requests for information that you will be asked to provide. This often needs to be done in a format specified by the target account. Many companies and local authorities choose this form of communication to give clarity to their requirements and maintain a high level of control on how this is done.

You are unlikely to be given an opportunity to present a completed tender in person. Target accounts use this process to define the terms and conditions to minimise the input from a supplier into the buying process. You might be given an opportunity to illustrate the benefits of your products, services and company at a formal presentation.

A tender can also include requests for information on your credit policy and environmental policy as well as any British and European standards or kite-marks. This can be needed to show a target account that your company conforms to agreed standards of work practice and service.

You are more likely to win a tender if you already have an existing relationship with the target account and can influence them as to what should be in it.

Structuring a quotation and a proposal

A quotation or proposal needs to be well constructed, as it will represent your offer to a potential buyer. Some degree of planning will be needed to ensure it is easy to read and relevant.

Try and choose either a neutral type font for either a quotation or proposal (like Arial), or one that the target account uses, so that you are communicating in a simple style. Also, consider using a type font that is large enough (say 12). This attention to detail will add value to what you are presenting.

Structure of a quotation

Try and think about what the recipient of your quotation/ proposal will expect to see to ensure that it meets his/her level of expectation. You should ensure that your work is clear, easy to read. You can structure a quotation in the following way:

STRUCTURING A QUOTATION

1 Introduction/needs analysis.

2 Your ability to meet need/requirement.

3 Your product/service and pricing offer.

4 Summary – *Linking benefits to your solution.*

Let us now look at an example of a quotation.

Example of a quotation

1 July 2003

Mr R Johnson
Sales and Marketing Director
IT Marketing Limited
1 George Street
London E1 123

Dear Richard

Thank you for the time extended to me recently. Further to our meeting I have pleasure in enclosing a quotation, which will meet your needs.

Needs analysis

Your needs

- 1.
- 2.
- 3.

Ability to meet needs

We can meet the above needs by providing a solution, which consists of:

- Link your solution to point 1.
- Link your solution to point 2.
- Link your solution to point 3.

Your pricing offer

Our offer

Product	Number of units	Service and maintenance	Price
A	5	£	£
B	10	£	£
C	15	£	£

VAT to be added to all prices quoted

Summary – benefit to customer

In summary, we can meet your needs and we feel that Products A, B and C will achieve this. Our offer will mean that you will be in a better position to fulfil your internal requirements. Our solution offers excellent value for money as it will save you time, improve your internal support system and reduce your need to use outside agencies.

I look forward to discussing this with you.

Yours sincerely

John Hall
Sales Executive
Tel: 020 7777 5555
Mob: 07970 123456
Email: jhall@xyz.com

NOTES:

In order to maintain the right level of politeness and professionalism when writing a quotation or a proposal, consider the following:

- Address your target person as Mr/Mrs/Miss/Ms – not first and last name only – E.g. Mr R Johnson, not Richard Johnson.

- If you are writing to a woman, find out if how she prefers to be addressed.

- If someone has professional qualifications, check if he/she prefers to have them included, e.g. Mr R Johnson Bsc.

- Always try and include someone's job title – it shows respect.

- Put your name and job title at the end of the correspondence.

- Including your mobile phone number at the end of your correspondence is optional.

- End a letter 'Yours sincerely' before signing it. (You would only use 'Yours faithfully' if you don't address the person you are writing to by his/her name.)

If you want to add any other company information, benefits or brochures, do this as a separate attachment to the actual quotation/proposal. This will allow buyers to look at this without detracting from the main document.

PRACTICAL POINTER

A quotation/proposal should not be a substitute for face-to-face selling or a presentation/demonstration of your products and services.

You should use the above template as a guide so that you can tailor quotations in your own style. This will also apply to a proposal which we are about to look at and will make it more relevant to you.

Structure of a proposal

The correct structure of a proposal will help make it easy to understand. When you are preparing, one remember to print a copy for other relevant key players in the account. Also, keep pricing information on a separate page as this will make it easier to find and to read.

A proposal should use a similar format to a quotation, but be more detailed in it's content. For example:

STRUCTURING A PROPOSAL

You can structure a proposal in the following way:

1   Introduction.

2   Needs analysis: *Confirmation of your target account's 'MUST HAVE' needs.*

3   Your ability to meet those needs.

4   Your product/service and pricing offer.

5   Supporting information/other benefits: *Environmental support and additional benefits = 'WOULD LIKE' needs.*

6   Summary.

It looks professional to place each of the above sections on a separate page. You can have a contents section at the beginning and number your pages. This is so that if someone you haven't met in the account is asked to look at it, he/she can easily find the relevant section. This adds clarity to your proposal.

Be careful not to confuse a presentation with a proposal. A presentation is based more on a summary/overview of your company and product benefits. It is also more likely to be produced in a PowerPoint format.

Try and choose a neutral type font for either a quote or proposal (like Arial), or one that the customer uses, so that you are communicating with them in a simple style. Consider using a type font that is large enough (say 12) so that your proposal is easy to read. This attention to detail will add value to what you are presenting.

If you don't meet all of the target account's needs, focus on what needs you can meet. Look at how your company provides the best overall solution and reinforce other areas of added value.

Let us now look at an example of a proposal to a company selling CRM solutions. They are looking for a way to help target accounts store customer information and to help improve communication. The aim of this is for the target account to retain their own customers and serve them better. Once again the above structure will be put in (BRACKETS) for this exercise.

Example of a sales proposal

Date:

Mr R Johnson
Sales and Marketing Director
IT Marketing Limited
1 George Street
London
E1 123

Dear Richard

Thank you for the time extended to me recently. Further to our meeting I have pleasure in enclosing a proposal, which will meet your needs.

I have covered this in the following way:

1   Introduction

2   Needs analysis

3   Our ability to meet your needs

4   Our offer

5   Additional benefits

6   Summary

I look forward to discussing this with you.

Yours sincerely

John Hall
Sales Executive
Tel: 020 7777 5555
Mob: 07970 123456
Email: jhall@xyz.com

Proposal to IT Marketing Limited

1 Introduction

As the increase in the demand for your company's products has developed, so has the need for improved storage of information. This will help you improve your communication with your prospects and customers. At present there is pressure on your marketing department in particular.

You also have a demand to store customer product information and give access to this to your outside sales consultants. After detailed research into a better contact management system, you have confirmed a need for the following requirements.

2 Summary of your needs – *Must have needs*

Your confirmed needs include a contact management system that can:

a. Have up to 10,000 customer contact records.

b. Integrate with Microsoft Outlook.

c. Track your outside sales consultants' appointments.

d. Filter customer information by postcode, annual spend etc.

e. Track customer preferences and meetings.

By doing this you recognise that you will serve your customers better and retain a higher proportion of them in the future.

3 Our ability to meet your needs

a. Have up to 10,000 customer contact records

We can provide a contact management solution that will allow you to store up to 20,000 records easily. This is significantly above your required specification and allows you room for growth in the years to come. It will also ensure that you can include information you need. For example:

- Customer name and address.
- Telephone, fax numbers, email addresses.
- Customer service records.
- Tracking customer buying trends/behaviour.

b. Integrate with Microsoft Outlook

You may wish to link a new system to Microsoft Outlook. This is because there are other parts of your organisation in the UK and Europe that use Outlook as the main contact management system. This need can be met and our software will make it easy to link the two.

c. Track your outside sales consultants' appointments

There is a need for you to have access to:

- marketing information that is sent out (in the form of mail shot campaigns); and
- marketing campaign information that is received (from your target accounts).

This information needs to be 'fed back' to your sales consultants and, where necessary, appointments with a new prospect need to be communicated to them and tracked.

We are able to achieve this and improve the communication your department has with your outside sales operation. You can store the marketing information you receive and include it in sales consultants' electronic diaries. This will enable them to retrieve the information remotely, on a daily basis.

By doing this you will be able to improve the efficiency of the marketing department as well as reduce the time sales consultants spend on the telephone receiving leads from your campaigns. This will improve the focus and effectiveness of their sales opportunities.

d. Filter customer information by postcode, annual spend etc

In order to manage existing marketing campaigns and introduce new ones, you have a need to be able to filter target account information. This needs to be done in the following way:

- By postcode.

- Town/City.

- Annual spend.

- Size of company.

- Number of employees.

- Job title.

Our software can achieve all of the above by doing a search upon request. A 'filter' is created that is easy to use. This will enable your marketing department and sales consultants to access key information quickly.

e. Track customer preferences and meetings

Your final main requirement was to track target accounts and customer preferences. This system will enable you to target and manage accounts more easily. The ability to do this better will improve your communication with these companies. You will also be able to use the diary management system to record telephone conversations as well as the outcome of meetings.

By using this aspect of our software you will improve your company's ability to stay at the forefront of your customers requirements. This will increase your sales potential and improve your customer retention. It will also allow other parts of your business to know the current status of an account and the actions that are being taken to grow your business in it.

4 Our offer

'Z' SOFTWARE

Product offer	Number of units	Total	Service (*Consultancy, maintenance and support*)	Total
'Z'	10	£	£	£
'Z'	20	£	£	£
'Z'	30	£	£	£

VAT to be added to all prices quoted

5 Other benefits of 'XYZ Limited' – Would Like Needs

EXPERIENCE

We have over ten years experience in offering contact management solutions. In that time we have successfully installed many systems that have helped companies similar to yours. Like you they have looked to improve their marketing support and communication.

LOCAL, NATIONAL AND EUROPEAN SUPPORT

This was an area that you wanted us to cover, although it is not a priority for you. We are located only 12 miles from your main UK offices, which means that if you do require extended maintenance and support, we are conveniently situated. We also have a National and European channel support network to help you maintain your systems at other ABC locations. This will give you guarantees of excellent after-sales support.

Account management focus

You liked the idea of quarterly review meetings to measure our progress in the account. These will give both IT Marketing and us an excellent opportunity to develop the business relationship.

We would welcome a discussion on which key personnel at ABC will need to be present. This is to ensure that our high level of after sales service to you is maintained throughout the life of your new system.

New product links

You showed an interest in this area for the future. As we introduce new product links to 'XYZ' software you will be able to have the option of adding these to your current system. If you decide to add new software licences we can do his as a download from the Internet or on a CD. The process is easy to install and ensures that you stay in touch with new technology. This will help you plan your marketing activity in the years to come.

We will also inform you in our review meetings of any new software that is applicable to your needs.

Service

Our after-sales service has recently been rewarded in 'Software Monthly' – the industry standard magazine for contact management system suppliers. To achieve this, the magazine had to do a controlled survey on fifty of our existing customers throughout the UK. The results showed that 97% of our users were 'very happy' with the system, our approach to business and our after sales support.

This type of endorsement should reassure you about our commitment to excellent customer service. "I will be delighted to supply references from existing customers should you require them."

6 Summary

In summary we are confident of being best placed to meet your contact management needs. We have built up much experience in the understanding of companies' marketing needs.

We are fully aware of how you propose to use the new system and we can support this. By having a better way of managing your sales opportunities you will:

- increase the chances of developing your target accounts; and

- increase customer retention.

We are confident that as your company grows, we can continue to contribute.

Additional information that can be added to a proposal

Additional information can also be added at the end of a proposal. This is information that supports your 'Must Have' and 'Would Like' needs. By leaving it until the end of the proposal (in a separate section) you are not confusing information that is *useful* with what is *essential*.

Some of the elements you could include information on are:

- Customer references/strong relationship with our your existing customers.

- Your relationship with a manufacturer (if you are a distributor).

- Other related products/services.

- Environmental accreditations.

- The history of your company.

- The benefits of your customer service team/technical department.

In terms of improving the actual proposal, you can enhance the presentation of it by:

- Scanning in the target account's logo, alongside your company's.

- Putting it in spot colour to add impact.

- Adding relevant PowerPoint slides (but not a complete presentation).

- Dividing the different proposal sections using coloured tabs/sheets.

- Including samples of your product.

- Including references/material to support your product/ service offering.

Ensure that your proposal is not too long and that it is relevant. It should be a proof statement for a target account that you understand their 'Must Have' needs in particular and can meet them. This will maintain the target account's focus on the areas of 'Commitment' as opposed to 'Interest'.

Writing quotations and proposals is easier if you have a structure and you remember to think about what you are looking to achieve. Your attention to detail will also have an impact on a target account. Your ability in these areas will help you to link a buyer's need to your solution. This will make it easier for target accounts to buy from your company.

Chapter summary

In this chapter we have looked at:

- Establishing that you are at proposal stage.
- Difference between quotes, proposals.
- Structuring a quote and a proposal.

We have looked at the need to confirm something in writing to a buyer. This should involve a summary of a buyer's commitment to a solution and a pricing structure. Writing quotations and proposals is challenging, as they require thought about structure and content. You need to look at the timing of each so that you do one at the right time and for the right reasons.

By doing this your written correspondence will reflect a buyer's needs and budget expectations. A good proposal, in particular, will impress a buyer and will help you to gain an edge over your competitors. It will confirm that you understand the target account's needs and can fulfil them.

Key points

✓ Ensure that you have the right level of commitment before you confirm your offer.

✓ Don't let written confirmation be a substitute for face-to-face selling.

✓ Structure your quotations and proposals so that they are easy to understand.

✓ Make sure that the target account's 'Must Have' needs have been met!

Coaching table

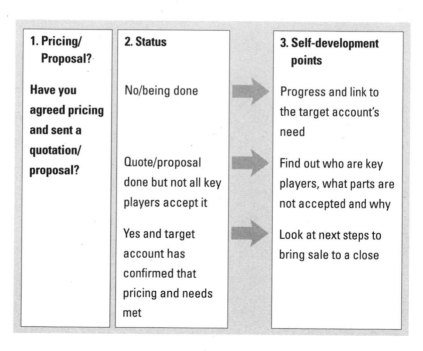

1. Pricing/ Proposal?	2. Status		3. Self-development points
Have you agreed pricing and sent a quotation/ proposal?	No/being done	→	Progress and link to the target account's need
	Quote/proposal done but not all key players accept it	→	Find out who are key players, what parts are not accepted and why
	Yes and target account has confirmed that pricing and needs met	→	Look at next steps to bring sale to a close

CHAPTER **EIGHT**

Negotiation

Negotiation

Introduction

If you have gained genuine commitment from a target account and presented your product/service and pricing solution, you will now be ready negotiate!

By the end of this chapter you will be able to:

- Become a good negotiator, rather than someone who only bargains

- Plan how to achieve a 'win – win' situation

- Know how to maintain your prices

- Understand what factors affect a negotiation

- Deal with different types of buyers and make them want to buy from you

Good negotiators protect their profit margin and achieve their sales objectives. This takes time, patience and skill.

Bargaining and negotiation

Before we look at the difference between bargaining and negotiation let us note some of the qualities of good negotiators. These include:

- Being knowledgeable about your products/services (and your market)
- Being a good listener
- Expressing yourself clearly
- Being patient (and having a relaxed manner)
- Being honest and 'customer focused'
- Being persuasive and decisive
- Know your target account's business/background

By showing these qualities you will be more relaxed and confident. This will then have a positive effect on the person you are negotiating with. Some people confuse the difference between bargaining and negotiation and bargaining. What are the differences?

Bargaining

Bargaining is the same as bartering. It is where one party wins a concession at the expense of the other. This is normally in the form of a price reduction! It has a major limitation in that the seller gets nothing in return for giving a concession.

If you sell in this style you will need to have a higher starting price than your actual selling price so that you can reduce it, without giving away too much price margin. Although this can give the impression to a buyer that your price was too high at the beginning. **It can also lead buyers to focus on price rather than value!**

Bargaining can illustrated in the following way:

Bargaining

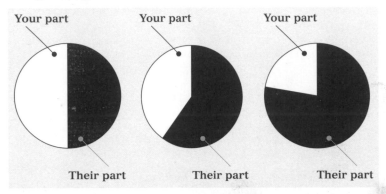

Negotiation

Negotiation is where both parties look to win through compromise. If the seller gives a concession, he/she will look for something from the buyer in return. **The focus here is on a 'win – win' situation.** For both parties, any concessions that are given are likely to be in a number of areas, other than price only. These include service, other products, length of agreement and future business potential.

The advantage of negotiation over bargaining is that the focus is not on price but on other areas of value! This is because, if a buyer wants a concession, he/she will be asked to concede something too. This encourages more of a partnership approach that leads to better long-term business relationships.

In a negotiation, the amount available to negotiate for both parties is larger than in bargaining. In the following chart, the seller is looking to bring into the negotiation items like the quantity of products purchased, length of agreement, future business and group discounting/price. The buyer looks to discuss topics like service, quality of the supplier's products, guarantees and price.

Areas of focus for a buyer and seller

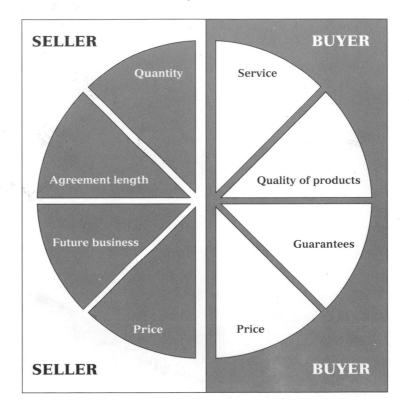

Price is not the only or dominant factor! Negotiation should result in an appreciation of one party, by the other. It also means that both parties will rarely finish where they started because they will need to be flexible and to adapt to the situation. However, the better negotiator you are, the easier it becomes to get the agreement you want. To do this you will need to plan how to achieve what you are looking for.

Setting out your objectives

Although many negotiations take place in an informal manner it is still a good idea to prepare. This will include getting to the appointment early enough to read through your objectives. By doing this you are likely to be more relaxed as you will have the main negotiation issues fresh in your mind.

Your objectives

When planning a negotiation, look at setting out your objectives, for example:

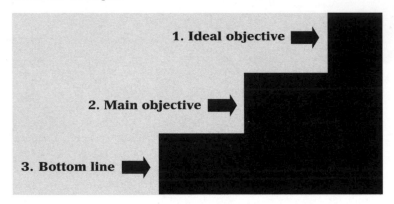

1   **Ideal**: Would like to achieve.

2   **Main objective**: Sacrifice some of the ideal objective to achieve this.

3   **Bottom line**: Only to be used if absolutely necessary.

To help you prepare, consider writing your objectives down before you begin a negotiation:

Your objectives

1 IDEAL OBJECTIVE:

_____

_____

2 MAIN OBJECTIVE:

_____

_____

3 BOTTOM LINE:

_____

_____

By focusing your attention on these principles you lessen your chances of giving away too much by concession. It is possible to have more steps, depending on the size/number of products involved, the length of your sales cycle and the company you are targeting. Avoid having to go to your bottom line. If you find that you are doing this focus harder on your areas of value.

A good way of looking objectively at an account before you go in to negotiate is to do a SWOT analysis. This analyses your:

- Strengths.
- Weaknesses.
- Opportunities.
- Threats.

This will enable you to recognise your own (and your company's) strengths as well as some of the weaknesses you will need to overcome and will help you to be aware of possible future business opportunities. It will also focus you on any potential threats from your competitors as well as key players in the target account itself.

The target account's objectives

As part of the preparation process you should look at what a buyer is likely to want. For example:

- What is the best outcome that you can expect and how can it be achieved?

- What would I do if I were in the buyer's position?

- What are the alternatives if you can't reach an agreement?

Consider listing the target account's objectives, for example:

Target account objectives

1 TARGET ACCOUNTS IDEAL OBJECTIVE:

_____

_____

2 MAIN OBJECTIVE:

_____

_____

3 BOTTOM LINE:

_____

_____

This preparation will help you to persuade a buyer of the value of reaching an agreement with you. Seeing things from a buyer's point of view will also give you an insight into his/her likely negotiating style. Planning is often the key to a win – win negotiation.

Areas of negotiation

Some negotiation areas will be more important to a buyer (and to you) than others. Therefore you will need to focus on what your distinguishing selling points (D.S.P's) are. This will enable you to reinforce your areas of added value and negotiate in those areas. These are the same ones we discussed in Chapter 2 – Targeting new accounts, (*Differentiating yourself from your competitiors*).

In the table below, we have created a list of D.S.P's (in the right hand column) to match each sales issue (in the left hand column).

Sales issues table

Negotiation and questioning areas	Distinguishing selling points
View of your company	• Experience • History
View of the competition	• Our competitive edge on product specification • Our nearer location
Products/services	• Product fit • Application

Negotiation and questioning areas	Distinguishing selling points
After sales service/support	• Specialist service team • Guarantees • Award winning service
Account management and business relationship needs	• Customer service team • Customer focus • My own history, experience and values • Referrals
Value for money	• Ability to meet your needs • Your agreement on product fit • Budget requirements able to be met
Other reasons	• Our professional standards – IS0 9001 • Guarantees

Setting out your objectives and planning are often the keys to a win – win negotiation. It will make it easier to see things from the buyer's perspective, which will give you an insight into his/her likely approach and position. This will help you to focus on the main issues that both parties will be looking to negotiate on.

The principles of negotiation

There are certain principles in negotiation with a target account that can help you to achieve your goals and close a sale successfully. These include:

- The value of your products/service.

- Your expected revenue and profit margin expectation.

- A buyer's timescale for making a decision.

- The price a target account wants to pay.

Negotiation can be made easier for you by linking a target account's 'Must Have' needs to your solution. You will also need to consider the following points:

1 Don't give a concession easily

The main rule to remember in negotiating is that:

'If you are asked to give a concession, ask for something back'.

A good negotiator will look at how a compromise can be reached to achieve this. It is important for both parties to feel that they have won a good proportion of what each set out to achieve.

2 Maintain your price levels

It can be tempting to reduce your price to try to get a quick sale! You may have to reduce your price but this should be as a last resort – not in the first instance! You should look at the type of accounts you are doing business with (and your own selling style) if they only seem interested in a low price!

There is a way of letting buyers know (without actually saying it), they are reaching your lowest offer. To do this:

- Make your first concession a reasonable one.

- Make your second much smaller.

- Make your third and any other concession even smaller.

For example if you have a total offer price of £5,000:

1st reduction – £4,850

2nd reduction – £4,800

3rd reduction – £4,780

Each of these concessions should warrant something being given back in return! If the buyer wants a fourth concession he/she can work out for themselves that it is only likely to give them about £10 off the last concession. By doing this, a buyer should question whether it is actually worth asking for another concession.

Continually reducing the prices of your product/service will give the wrong impression to a buyer. This is something that you don't want, particularly if you are selling the latest technology or something that you have offered as 'high value' to the target account.

Maintaining your price will have a positive psychological effect on a buyer and strengthen your negotiating position.

3 Look at the wider picture

Always keep the entire business proposition in mind. Knowing your target account's requirements in full will strengthen your negotiating position. This will help you to:

- Reinforce the value of your products and services

- Focus the value in the buyer's mind

It will also help to focus the buyer on the benefits of a long-term business relationship.

4 Look at the value of a concession

If you have to give a concession, look to choose something that has a low value to you but a high value to the buyer, (like free delivery). This will help you protect your profit margin.

5 Stand firm

If buyers look for a concession remember to justify your offer. If you give a concession too quickly, you might give the impression that there are others worth looking for.

6 The danger of deadlines

A deadline can focus a buyer's attention on the close date and encourage them to make a decision. If you decide to set a deadline for a particular product/service, stick to it and make it realistic. This can happen on special offers/marketing campaigns. If you don't, you will give buyers the impression that it was not genuine. You could appear too keen to win their business, which can encourage buyers to look for other concessions.

If buyers put a deadline on something, this can have a positive and negative effect for you:

- **Positive** – Because it focuses their attention on a defined timeframe.

- **Negative** – Because they may expect concessions before the deadline.

Try to get an agreement regarding any deadline that is imposed on you. This will ease the pressure on both parties, making an agreement more likely.

7 Negotiate the deadlock

If you reach deadlock you will need to confirm the areas that you do and don't agree on and get an understanding of why this is. By now, both you and the buyer will probably have invested much time and effort. Go back in the sales cycle and

re-emphasise the points that you agree on so that a compromise can be found.

8 Be aware of the strengths and weaknesses of your offer

If a buyer thinks that there is a weakness in your offer, try and isolate it. As opposed to reducing your price, look to minimise an objection by:

- Reinforcing the value added areas.

- Changing the offer.

- Linking your offer to the buyer's overall needs.

This will help you to focus a buyer on your solution being the right one.

9 Confrontation

If you find yourself becoming confrontational take 'a step back'. This type of scenario creates a 'lose – lose' situation. If a buyer becomes confrontational try and pacify the situation by looking for areas of common agreement.

You should avoid getting into this situation in the first place! You cannot win an argument with a buyer! If this situation occurs, goodwill breaks down which will need to be repaired before a successful negotiation can be concluded. You will need patience and good interpersonal skills to focus the buyer on how both parties can 'win' out of the situation.

The principles of negotiation take practice. Learn from any mistakes you or the buyer make. You can do this by reviewing each sales call and being honest with yourself about how it went. This will help you get better at reacting to any concessions a buyer requests. Also, by focusing on the value of your solution, you will make it easier for a 'win – win' outcome to happen.

Understanding the person you are selling to

When you are going to negotiate with a buyer remember to prepare. When you are preparing to negotiate with a target account, it is wise to understand the type of buyer you are likely to meet. This will help you work out a strategy of the best way to sell.

Pressures on both parties

The negotiation stage can potentially be a stressful time for both buyer and seller. This is because of the time taken since you first met and began discussing future business. Also, both parties realise that the time is coming when a decision has to be made.

(This will depend on the length of your sales cycle and how well you have got to know the target account).

For a buyer, it could be a time when he/she might be judged internally on how good a winning supplier is. It could also involve telling at least one supplier that their hard work has not been successful on this occasion!

Let us look at the main types of buyer you are likely to meet and their main negotiation focus.

Different types of buyer

In a negotiation, buyers will have different types of personality and experience. However, the four main considerations that they tend to focus on are:

1 Business needs and objectives.

2 Price/facts and figures.

3 Products/service/3rd party references.

4 The customer/supplier relationship.

Good buyers (at all managerial levels) will focus on *all* of these areas. This is likely to be affected by the role they have in their company and other people involved in the decision-making process. For example, a Finance Director's main concern will be the second factor – Price/facts and figures.

Adapting your sales style

You should try to know what likely area of interest a buyer will focus on and how to react to it. By doing this you increase your chances of doing business with the account. Let us look at the four areas (opposite) of buyer focus/interest in a negotiation and how you should react to it.

Buying focus

Buyer focus	Buyer's likely areas of interest	Reacting to different types of buyer
1 Business needs and objectives	• Your solution versus other suppliers • Justification of product fit • What benefits a solution brings • Fitting in with the business objectives	• Stick to the objectives • Be prepared and well organised • Have supporting information • Relate your solution to the business objectives
2 Price/ facts and figures	• The cost of your products/ services • Budget restrictions • Timing/flexibility • Cost effective options	• Have financial information to support your arguments • Be prepared to discuss figures • Break down your proposal • Prove that you offer value for money

Buyer focus	Buyer's likely areas of interest	Reacting to different types of buyer
3 Products/ service/ 3rd party references	• The application of your products/service • Comparisons between existing and new methods • After sales guarantees	• Ensure product/service meet needs • Gap between existing situation and proposed solution • Meet the product/service specification • Reinforce relia-bility/referrals
4 The customer/ supplier relationship	• Account management issues/reviews • Future guaran-tees on supplier loyalty • Development of the business relationship	• Your own level of professionalism/ experience • Your company's reputation/ history • Understanding target account's needs • Partnership approach • Future business opportunities

Knowing the type of buyer you are going to negotiate with will help you focus on what issues are important to him/her. This will put you in a better negotiating position by making it easier for a buyer to trust you.

PRACTICAL POINTER

Trust is a key element in a negotiation that will encourage buyers to want to do business with you.

Knowing the 'culture' of a target account is another consideration. This will require you understanding something about their values, products/services and market. (As looked at in Chapter 2 – Targeting new accounts, (*Background information on a new account*.))

Knowing how to sell to different types of buyer will help you to negotiate more easily. It will also make it easier for a target account to buy from you.

Chapter summary

In this chapter we have looked at:

- Bargaining and negotiation.

- Setting out your objectives.

- The principles of negotiation.

- Understanding the person you are selling to.

It is important for both parties to have a 'win – win' situation. This is more likely to be achieved by focusing on negotiating rather than bargaining because a negotiation involves looking for something in return for giving a concession. By setting out your objectives you will be able to think about your strategy and that of a buyer.

Understanding the principles of negotiation will help you deal with different types of situations. Finally, understanding the type of focus a buyer is likely to have will help you to know how to react in order to maximize your profit margin.

Key points

✓ Understand the difference between bargaining and negotiation.

✓ Focus on a 'win – win' situation and value, not merely on price.

✓ Set out your objectives (and look at this from a buyer's point of view).

✓ Practice the principles of negotiation – they will improve your position.

✓ Understand the type of buyer you will be negotiating with.

Coaching table

1. Negotiation?	2. Status		3. Self-development points
Are you in negotiations with the target account?	No	→	Look at timing/commitment you have from the target account
	Yes, but there is no/limited commitment to a decision	→	Find out what/who is holding up the decision and why
	Yes	→	Look for areas of agreement, get commitment and close

CHAPTER **NINE**

Closing the sale

Closing the sale

Introduction

During a negotiation, you will be looking at ways to 'close the sale'. Winning an order should be the most rewarding part of the sales process. It is the result of the hard work and determination that has been put in with a target account.

By the end of this chapter you will be able to:

- Develop good closing techniques.

- Be flexible in the types of close that you use.

- Understand more about different buying signals.

- Look at how to overcome common objections.

Being flexible in your approach can help you and this begins with using different types of closing technique.

Different types of 'Close'

When you close a sale there are a number of ways in which you can ask for an order. By being familiar with different types of 'close' you will be in a better position to decide which one to use. This will help you to adapt to the situation and differentiate you from someone that uses the same close on every occasion.

By using 'hard' closing techniques you will come across as too forceful or insensitive. By not closing at all (or in a weak manner), you could appear unassertive or not being interested in the order. A close can change in meaning depending on your tone and body language. You should therefore try to select the appropriate one, at the right time and in the right manner.

Let us look at the most common types of close. They are:

The 'Direct' close

The 'Direct' close is the most common type. It is when you ask for an order directly, e.g. "Can I have the order".

The 'Alternative' close

The 'Alternative' close is when you give a buyer a choice of one option or another. It focuses the buyer on two possible alternatives, both of which offer your solution e.g. "Will you be ordering Product X or Product Y?"

The 'Assumptive' close

This is when you assume that the buyer wants to go ahead; he/she may have given you this impression without actually saying so. e.g. "When would you like our delivery to take place?"

The 'Half Nelson' close

This close has to be used in the right context, as it is associated with a more forceful closing style, e.g. "If I can match that price, can I have the order?" It is similar to the 'Direct' close, but precedes it with a closed question. It needs to be used in the right context so that a buyer does not feel 'pushed' into signing an order.

Cost benefit analysis

This close looks at asking a buyer to list the reasons for and against choosing your products/services or company to do business with! You will want to give help in support of your offer and no/limited help for the reasons against it!

It can also be useful in finding out whether (in a buyer's eyes), you have overcome all of his/her objections regarding a particular issue.

A trial

This method offers target accounts the opportunity to try out your product/service before a sale takes place so that they feel an obligation to buy it.

Buyers knows that it can be returned, but once they get used to it, the hope is that this becomes increasingly unlikely. This close has to be used carefully to ensure that you don't offer trials on products as a substitute for getting genuine commitment!

The 'Sympathy' close

This is where you use sympathy from buyers to try and influence their decision. You appeal to their loyalty or sense of fairness. It can be used effectively by appealing to a buyer to accept your solution. However, used in the wrong context a sales person may come across as weak or indecisive and can reduce the value of your offer.

The 'Lost Sale' close

The 'Lost Sale' close is used after a buyer has told you that you have lost an order. By asking the question – "Where did I go wrong", you might get the opportunity to understand why and then perhaps be able to go back in the sales cycle to overcome the objection. This is a high risk – often, low return strategy. By using it you might not have developed a sale correctly earlier in the cycle!

The 'Deadline' close

This close gives buyers a deadline or timeframe to encourage them to make a decision, e.g. "The offer ends soon" or "This is the last available stock left". It can be effective, especially with promotions. However, you will need to ensure that the deadline is genuine so that a buyer doesn't ignore it or feel pressurised by it. If this happens it can be counter productive.

The 'Referral' close

This is where you refer to other companies who have had similar experience, e.g. "ABC Limited were in a similar position to you and by using our products they were able to solve that issue."

These closes will need practice to ensure that they are delivered in a in a way you feel comfortable with. This will help you to appear natural. If it is done well it should make buyers feel relaxed which will have a positive effect on them.

PRACTICAL POINTER

A golden rule in closing a sale is that once you have asked a closing question – **don't speak until the buyer has answered!**

If you keep talking, you could talk yourself out of a sale. Buyers must have an opportunity to think and convince themselves that this is the end of the sale. By not interrupting a buyer at this critical time you increase your chances of either:

- getting the order; or

- finding out why a buyer doesn't want to proceed.

If you do interrupt a buyer, you are more likely to receive an objection because you haven't given that person the time to think clearly.

However good you are at closing, you will also need to manage other elements that affect you – interpreting buying signals and overcoming objections.

Buying signals and overcoming objections

When you are negotiating there will be a number of possible issues that buyers will want to discuss. These could include your products, services, prices etc. It is therefore important to:

Understand what buyers say and what they mean!

At the negotiation stage buyers may be reluctant to reveal their true feelings in case this is used by a sales person to gain an advantage. So, you will need to interpret their words and their body language to help you.

For example, when a buyer says – "This is not something we would normally accept", what he/she could mean is – "Convince me"!

Other buying-signals might include:

Buyer: "I'd rather not negotiate prices today"

"I am prepared to negotiate other aspects of your offer (and I will soon be ready to discuss price)"

Buyer: "You're too expensive"

"I would like a concession, or you need to justify the value of your offer before I will agree to it"

Buyer: "I couldn't order that much in one delivery"

"But I might be prepared to over a period of time, or if you hold the stock"

Buyer: "I can't sign off that amount"

I need to get approval (probably from my immediate manager)

To be good at reading buying-signals you will need to use your listening skills and intuition and experience. You will need to decide whether an objection is genuine, a buying-signal or a request for a concession. By doing this you will make it easier to get agreement.

Overcoming objections

When closing a sale, getting an objection can be a sign that a buyer is interested. However, if you get objections consistently it could be a sign of indifference or lack of interest! In this case it is more likely that you have not developed the sale properly or are closing too early.

Have respect for buyers. Don't waste their time and ensure that they don't waste yours! This can be achieved by knowing the type of person you are dealing with and ensuring you have agreed objectives and parameters. You should also ensure that you have understood the target account's decision-making process.

PRACTICAL POINTER

Put your emphasis on objection prevention rather than having to overcome them. This can be achieved by getting the buyer/decision-maker's agreement at each stage of the sales cycle and covering the 'sales issues' well.

When offering a solution, be careful not to describe what your products and services do without including the benefits to the buyer, (as looked at in Chapter 5 – Developing a sale correctly (*Presenting the benefits of your solution*)) – you are more likely to increase a buyer's concern with price and encourage unnecessary objections.

Many objections are caused by a solution being provided too early in the sale.

Ideally, in this situation you should look to develop interest and turn it into commitment. If not, you are more likely to get a buyer to raise objections, which you might read as buying signals! This will not help you!

When closing, if you do get an objection, try and establish if it is:

- **A genuine objection** (when a buyer has a real issue); or

- **A false objection** (when a buyer is looking for a concession)!

In this situation, ask the buyer a question to get clarification. This will help you understand why the objection has arisen. If you do get an objection that you can't overcome don't try and close a sale without overcoming it. If you do it will either lessen your chances of a sale or encourage a buyer to look for a price reduction.

- Go back in the sales cycle.

- Look at the reason why the objection has arisen.

- Overcome it.

- Close.

If you can't overcome it you will have to reinforce the value of your offer and focus a buyer on the overall business benefits. Let us now look at some of the most common objections you are likely to get and how to overcome them.

Common objections

1. PRICE

- Find out what price the buyer was expecting to pay.

- Focus on the difference in the price rather than the price itself.

- Counter with value.

- Give examples of how a target account will benefit from paying your asking price.

- Offer to negotiate.

2. BUYER NOT CONVINCED

- Isolate the problem/issue.

- Ensure that the buyer has been taken through sales cycle properly.

- Go back and check the buyer's understanding.

- Clarify key points.

- Show action and look for commitment.

3. NO/LIMITED BUDGET

- Go back and find out how this has come about.

- Get confirmation on budget.

- Offer stepped payments/finance – not a price reduction!

- Find out what budget is available/when a budget will be in place.

- Find out if your solution is costing more than target account wants to pay.

- Involve the budget holder (and immediate manager/finance director).

4. I'VE BEEN DEALING WITH YOUR COMPETITOR FOR YEARS

- Isolate the areas they like about the competitor – then match/beat them!

- Get commitment on the buying criteria and your company/product/service benefits.

- Isolate areas that need improvement/adapt your offer to focus more on these.

- Give references/guarantees as a proof statement.

- Show empathy but then try and help a buyer reinforce the proposed change.

5. DELIVERY

- Compare delivery with the overall benefits.

- Isolate this concern and compare it with the target account's 'Must Have' needs.

- Try to focus on the positive aspects.

- Reinforce the benefits of your products, company and service.

6. A SECOND OPINION

- Meet someone else involved in the buying decision.

- Isolate areas of agreement.

- Build up the buyer's confidence in you – focus on your main benefits.

- Look to set up another meeting to discuss the outcome (of a second opinion).

7. I WANT TO SEE THE COMPETITION

- Don't fear this as it could devalue a buyer's confidence in your company.

- Ask why this is now necessary and what the buyer wants to see.

- Check that you have progressed the sales properly.

- Focus on how your product/service meets the target account's need.

- Find out if this is a genuine objection or the request for a concession.

- Reinforce your consultative approach.

- Make an appointment to see buyer after a competitor has been seen.

8. I WANT TO THINK ABOUT IT

- Find out why a buyer needs to do this.

- Make another appointment (to take the pressure off).

- Don't pressurise buyers – guide them.

- Use your questioning techniques to uncover the need to delay.

- Find out if something has changed.

- Make sure that the buyer is convinced of the merits of your product or service.

Objections are normally a sign that a buyer is not totally convinced about an aspect of your offer. They can also be given by a buyer for negotiation purposes to get another concession from you. Good salespeople don't fear objections; they look to overcome any concerns or doubts a buyer might have. By developing a sale well at each stage you will lessen the number of objections you get.

Good closing techniques

Closing a sale should be natural. Both parties should have come to a point where more negotiation will not lead to any further concessions being given by either party. At this time, buyer and seller will have achieved most of the gains that they were looking for. Both sides will have had to concede some ground in order to arrive at an agreement.

Develop a sale properly before you close

This can be a challenging time for both parties because they may have spent weeks or months getting to this stage. Both could be asking themselves – "Have I got the best deal I could have? Is there anything that I have missed?" Therefore, the timing of closing a sale needs to be considered.

When you are looking to close a sale, the more closes you do can lessen your chances! This is because some salespeople substitute effective needs analysis and development for closing techniques. If you have not developed a sale properly, buyers might think that you are pushing them. This is more likely to lead them to not buying or to ask for a price reduction. This will be due to their lack of commitment/perceived value in your solution.

Don't let closing techniques be a substitute for good selling!

When you want to close a sale don't ask too many closed questions. This may lead to the buyer feeling pressurised and resistance could indicate that they have not bought into your solution. Conversely, not closing at all will lead to the buyer becoming frustrated or feeling that the negotiations are still on going. This will give an advantage to your competitors.

If you have done a good job in developing the buyer's needs, you will have earned the right to close for an order. When closing remember to:

1 Cover all of the buyer's 'Must Have' needs

2 Link these to your benefits

3 Summarise

4 Ask for a commitment

Therefore, developing a sale well will make closing easier for both parties.

Troubleshooting

In some negotiations, you will not be able to get a decision when you are with the buyer. This could be because a target account:

- Wants to involve other key players without your input

- Has a corporate buying policy/decision-maker

- Has a head office decision-maker (who is located outside your territory)

- Is part of another company/a subsidiary

If you have to involve other colleagues of your company in helping to develop a sale or close a deal, stay involved! Your own management should encourage this. By doing so your company will benefit from your understanding of the target account's needs at a local level.

Another possibility is that you have to wait for a decision involving other key players in the account. This can be frustrating because the next 'move' will come from them.

If the waiting time becomes too long, what can you do? You can ask for an update/close date, or think of a reason to contact the account. This can be high risk and should be used only if an agreed time period has elapsed. It can be done if you feel that by delaying an advantage swings towards a competitor.

Reasons to contact a buyer in this situation might include:

- Asking if anything has changed since your last meeting

- Checking that the buyer's views/needs are still the same

- Checking that certain 'key players' understand/prefer your solution

- Asking when a final decision is likely

- Introduce a new (but relevant/genuine) piece of information

The reason for a call like this is to find out what decision a target account is likely to make. Your aim at this late stage is to find out if there is anything you can do to influence it.

Let us now look at an exercise to reinforce your understanding of closing a sale.

Closing the sale

Question	True	False
1 The more you use closing techniques during a call, the more often a target account will buy		
2 Closing techniques work best earlier in the sale when you are selling low value goods or trying to get a very small commitment from the customer		
3 Never take the initiative by asking the buyer for commitment, always let the sale close itself		
4 There's only one thing worth closing for in a sales call and that's an order for your product/service		
5 When closing, you should check that you've covered the buyer's needs, linked them to the benefits and obtained a commitment		
6 Objections are a sign that a buyer is interested; so the more objections you get, the better your chances of making a sale		

7 By focusing on what your products/services do, rather than the benefits they offer, you will increase a buyer's concern with price		
8 The more you describe what your products/services do, the fewer objections you will receive		
9 If you can make 'benefits' during the call you are likely to receive support and agreement from a buyer rather than objections		
10 Developing 'Would Like' needs so that they become 'Must Have' needs will reduce the number of objections a buyer has		

ANSWERS:

1 **False**: Closing too early in a sale can put a buyer off!

2 **True**: This is because the sales cycle is short/benefits more easily understood

3 **False**: You can't rely on a buyer to want to close/direct the sale

4 **False**: Other reasons could be – next appointment, presentation etc.

5 **True**: By doing this you ensure that you have developed the call correctly

6 **False**: They can highlight a buyer's concern/lack of commitment

7 **True**: Buyers won't easily understand how your product will benefit them

8 **False**: A buyer is more likely to become bored with this approach

9 **True**: This is because buyers will relate your benefits to their needs

10 **True**: This will ensure that you have turned 'interest' into 'commitment'

Whatever the situation, you should always act in a professional and honest manner. Look at the time you spend on a target account and analyse the potential of the business you are looking to gain. Assess how good a sales opportunity it is and how long it will take to develop. To ensure that you have developed a sale well, look at the forecasting issues in Chapter 1 – Preparation and sales development (*Forecasting future sales*).

Remember to be flexible and be yourself – you are more likely to be effective if you do this, and close a sale more easily. You won't win business in all target accounts, but you will increase your chances.

Good closing techniques will help you to win future business. Put your efforts into objection prevention by trying not to close a sale too early. This will reduce the number of objections you will get and make it easier to close a sale.

Chapter summary

In this chapter we have looked at:

- Different types of 'Close'.
- Buying signals and overcoming objections.
- Good closing techniques.

Using different types of close will make you flexible. This will relax a buyer, making the close of a sale a natural conclusion for both parties. We have looked at the difference between what buyers say and what they can mean. Interpreting buying-signals will make it easier to overcome any objections from a buyer. If you do get an objection clarify whether it is genuine or false.

This will help you to determine if a buyer is using it as a way to gain a concession.

Good closing techniques will focus you on objection prevention. By applying these principles at the right time, more target accounts will buy from you.

Key points

✓ Try different closes, it will give you flexibility and confidence.

✓ Understand the difference between what buyers say and what they mean!

✓ When you close for an order ALWAYS let the buyer speak next!

✓ Think about the type of objections you could get and how to overcome them.

✓ Don't let closing techniques be a substitute for good selling!

Coaching table

1. Closing appointment	2. Status		3. Self-development points
Do you have an appointment to close the sale?	No/not yet	→	Understand the reasons why and progress the sale
	Not ready yet/looking to make one	→	Summarise your status in the account and get commitment for a close date
	Yes	→	Ensure that you are prepared and ready to overcome any objections

CHAPTER **TEN**
**Managing your accounts and
your sales performance**

Managing your accounts and your sales performance

Introduction

Closing a sale successfully is the target that every sales professional works towards. It is the 'pay off' for the hard work that has been put in throughout a sale. When this has been done and your products and services are in place, a new relationship begins. This is where a target account becomes a customer!

We will now look at how you can manage business relationships in new and existing accounts. We will also focus on how you can analyse your own sales performance to look at how you can develop yourself in a number of areas.

By the end of this chapter you will be able to:

- Look at accounts in an objective way to reduce the time of the sales cycle.

- Understand the type of information you need to achieve this.

- Develop a strategy to win business/grow an account.

- Monitor your sales performance in order to become more effective.

These disciplines will enable you to manage your accounts better and can be shared with your own sales manager/directors to help you sell more. The first part of this is to look at the target account's contacts and your distinguishing selling points.

Managing target accounts and relationships

By managing a target account well, whether it is new or existing, you will help to differentiate your company from your competitors. This will make it easier to introduce new products and services into the account and develop other business relationships. It will also build confidence and trust in you as an account manager.

PRACTICAL POINTER
Trust is a key part of any customer/supplier relationship.

This was highlighted in Chapter 9: Negotiation, (*Understanding the person you are selling to*).

Target account information

One of the factors that can help to develop the account relationship is the number of people you know who might influence a sale. A way of focusing your attention in this area is to break down your contacts into those that you know and ones that you would like to get to know. Sometimes, you might know a role exists but not know that person's name or vice versa.

To do this effectively, break down the level of contact into three areas:

1   **Senior management** – Board Directors and senior managers.

2   **Middle management** – Middle Managers and budget holders.

3   **Influencers** – People who have no budget responsibility, but input into the buying process – Assistants, Supervisors, Administrators etc.

This was defined in the introduction, (Glossary of sales terms) and can be illustrated in the following way:

Target account contacts

Account: ABC Limited	Date:	
Level of Contact	**Known contacts** (+ title)	**Relevant contacts** yet to meet (+ title)
Senior Management *MD, Any Board Director, senior manager*	**James Lambert** Purchasing Director	**Simon Jones** Managing Director **Sarah Johnson** Finance Director
Middle Management Purchasing/Office/ Facilities Manager, Buyer	**Sean Davies** Purchasing Manager **Lynne Fynnes** Office Manager	**Name unknown** Facilities Manager **Sy Ranan** IT Manager
Influencer level Assistant, P, Supervisor Administrator, PA	**Sol Razman** Purchasing Assistant **Janice Ronan** P.A. to J Lambert	**John Dane** IT (Title unknown) **Name unknown** Network specialist

Ideally you should get to know someone at each level. This will increase your knowledge of the account and your level of influence making it easier to gain support in future decision-making.

Some contacts influence a buying decision later in the sales process or once a target account has become a customer. Also, if a competitor has a good relationship with someone in a target account that you don't know (or know well) it can make it harder to get that person's approval to your solution.

Try to find out all the 'key players' involved in the buying process before the beginning of a sale. In new accounts much of this will depend on your main contact's desire for you to meet different people in the account! You will need to sell the benefits to your main contact to achieve this. Investigating the target account's buying process can help.

The sales issues

In many target accounts you will need to understand their business issues. This can be done by creating a 'sales issues table' of D.S.P's – (Distinguishing Selling Points) table, similar to the one in Chapter 2 – Targeting new accounts, (Differentiating yourself from your competitors). The difference between the two is that this table focuses on your competitor's selling points, not your own.

Target account – Distinguishing selling points

Account name:	Date:
THE SALES ISSUES – D.S.P. areas	

View of their company:

- Trading for over thirty years – experience.
- Strength and knowledge of their people.
- Growth by acquisition.

View of the competition:

- They have two leading competitors – Company X and Company Y.
- Have specialised role in their market.
- Have focused more on domestic market than their main competitors.

Products/services:

- Large product offering.
- New product range has given them an edge this year.
- Tailored service offering.

After sales Service/Support:

- Fast response times.
- National network distribution.
- History of good after sales service.

Account management/business relationship needs:

- Account managers who place importance of customer satisfaction.
- More service personnel compared with competitors.
- High investment in training and developing their staff.

Value for money:

- They offer competitive products and services.
- 2002 Winner of 'Supplier of the year' award in their market.
- Largest growth in UK last year.

Other D.S.P's:

- Only company to continually invest in UK (when other competitors have down sized).
- Use 'Call Centre' for customer service – unlike competitors, this has speeded-up response times to customers.

Knowing something about a target's accounts market and business strategy can help you gain credibility. Your selling skills should also impress a buyer (at any managerial level). How much time you invest in this area will of course depend on your sales role, your main contact and the value of any potential/existing business opportunities.

You will need to determine how much information you should know about a target account when you start developing it. Often, the larger the sale you are managing, the more important knowing something about the account will be.

Developing an account strategy

Developing an account properly is an important part of growing your own revenue and profit potential. Eighty per cent of most companies turnover comes from only twenty per cent of their customers, (known as the Pareto principle). This is why it is important you win a new account, you keep it!

The benefits of good account management are:

- It helps you to develop business relationships and the right accounts.

- It enables you to understand how key players interact with each other.

- It will help you to prioritise on accounts and manage your time well.

- It will differentiate you from your competitors.

- It sets a standard for developing an account properly.

- It usually takes more time and effort to win a new account.

Understanding an account's needs essential if you are going to win business in it. This will involve having the right type of information at your disposal.

Developing an account profile

It normally takes much time and effort to win a new account. Having a way of managing its development will focus you in the right areas and make you more effective. To help this process write down what your objectives are and how you think they can be achieved. This will give you a better idea of a new or existing account's potential. It will also enable you to discuss the account's development with your management and relevant colleagues.

Let us look at how you can build up an account profile in order to manage your own target accounts better. Any account profile your company develops should be able to have a link with your company database. This will make it easier for internal communication purposes.

As an example, we will complete two out of many possible sections that make up a completed profile. Other areas that you could add are listed so that you can tailor this to your own company's needs.

Part 1 looks at:

ACCOUNT INFORMATION

This requires you to list the name of the account and supporting information.

BUSINESS POTENTIAL

This section asks you to describe briefly the existing account situation and list any sales potential.

Part 2 looks at:

CONTACT NAMES AND ATTITUDES

This is where the 'key players' titles, managerial level, location and attitude are listed. You should indicate the number (and possibly type) of meetings you have had so far and any future ones planned. Any 'key player' who has not yet been met should also be listed.

Part 1 - *Account information and business potential*

Account Profile

Account information	Business potential

Account Manager: John Langer

Account information

Account name *ABC Limited*
& location: London EC1

Type of Business? Network Printing

Existing or New A/C? New

Account status: Shared account

Main competitor: XYZ Limited

Today's date:

Close date?

Business potential

Possible products:

> Product A   Price X

> Product B   Price Y

> Service contract   Price Z

>

Amount of revenue potential?   **TOTAL**

Summary of situation: Customer wants to add new printer to Oxford location

Part 2 - Contact names and attitudes

Account Profile

Account Manager: John Langer

Business potential

Account name *Citycore services*
& location: London EC1

Type of Business? Network Printing
Existing or New A/C? New
Account status: Shared account
Main competitor: XYZ Limited
Today's date:
Close date?

Possible products:

> CVC 200 — Price X
> RIP — Price Y
> Additional software — Price Z
>

Amount of revenue potential? — **TOTAL**

Summary of situation: Customer wants to add new printer to Oxford location

Contact name & title	Level	Location	Contact attitude	Examples	Meetings
				Sees benefit?	
Jenny Morgan - Purchasing Director	Senior mgt	London	?/Decision Maker	Ex/inexperienced?	None
				Would prefer delay?	
Rav Simmonds - Purchasing Mgr	Middle mgt	Oxford	Pro solution/Has budget	? = Don't know	3 since last Qtr (re. Budget)
				Pro solution	
John Bolton - IT operator	Influencer	Oxford	Pro solution/positive	Positive / Negative	3 since last Qtr
				Pro competition	
Susan Thomas - Finance Director	Senior mgt	London	?/Experienced	Budget concerns	None
				Decision maker?	

You can add to this by looking at other target account issues. These include:

THE CURRENT POINT IN SALES CYCLE

This would confirm why you and/or a competitor are a supplier and the timeframes of present/future business.

SALES SUPPORT INFORMATION

This part would ask questions relating to information about the account. For example:

- Have service issues been covered?

- Has a presentation been done?

This will give you a better understanding of what is needed to support and monitor the current sales activity.

ISSUES/CHALLENGES AND SOLUTIONS

You can list:

- Current issues affecting the development of the account.

- Who has confirmed them.

- Your solutions to them.

- When they will be solved and by whom.

Issues that need to be solved can come from within your company as well as the target account.

Ensure that your contact confirms a situation, don't assume something if you don't know or are not sure.

You will need to probe contacts in the account to confirm your understanding of how to develop it well. This will help you to minimise the chances of making a mistake.

Actions needed to progress the sale/relationship

Try to identify any additional information that could affect the development of a sale or the account in general. Commit yourself and others in the account to a timeframe for these actions to be completed. Get agreement from your own colleagues involved in supporting you, so that some tasks are communicated, shared and delegated properly. Don't abdicate responsibility, as this will reduce your chances of developing the account well.

Forecast of current opportunities

You can also include a current forecast of business in the account profile like timeframe, budget, product fit etc. as looked at in Chapter 1 – Targeting new accounts, (*Forecasting future sales*). This can ensure that you focus on the forecasting issues and develop the business potential in the account properly.

Measuring partnership potential

You can also adapt the forecasting model to give priority to different types of target account and measure the partnership potential. Creating a compatibility table can do this. This would involve picking five different topics that can be graded (in columns) in the same way as a forecasting model. In order to keep it simple, ensure that the total someone could score is one hundred; this enables it to be illustrated as a percentage.

For example:

- Partnership potential.

- Budget.

- Service issues.

- Timescale and need.

- Product/service compatibility.

This can be illustrated in the following way (*see opposite*):

Compatibility table

Account: ? **Account Manager:** ? **Date:** ?

Rating	Partnership /Added value	Budget/price	Service	Time-scale and need	Product / account compatibility
0%	Isn't looking for partnership/See no added value in doing so	Negative status	Negative status	Negative status	Negative status
10%	Middle management have confirmed need to build partnership/See added value in doing so	Neutral status	Neutral status	Neutral status	Neutral status
20%	Senior management have confirmed need to build partnership/See added value in doing so	Positive status	Positive status	Positive status	Positive status
Your score	10%	Column score %	Column score %	Column score %	Column score % 10 %

Senior management = **Directors** - (Managing, sales, finance, production, marketing, purchasing + chief executive - Delegates authority to Middle management
Middle management = **Managers** - (Facilities, Purchasing, Training, IT etc. - Probable Decision-Maker controller of a budget)
Influencers = **Assistant** - (supervisor, office services manage, Assistant - non budget holder)

NB. Larger companies will have more than three layers of management. Middle managers often have control of a budget.

Below 50% = Either this is not a top priority or much work is needed for this account to do business with you
50 – 70% = You have some good potential for medium term business (3 - 6 months)
70%+ = The account has good short-term potential and should be a key focus for account development

Focusing on accounts that have the most potential will help you to see above your accounts and manage your time efficiently.

Having an account strategy will make it easier for you to break into and maintain an account. It can involve knowing a number of different people; often with different management levels. Developing your own account profile with relevant information in it can support this. This will help you and others in your company communicate better and remain objective about its development.

Gaining an advantage

When a target account makes a decision to choose a supplier it is often a number of key things done well that make a difference. This happens at different stages of the sales cycle. Suppliers that do this successfully gain a competitive advantage, even if their product/service offering is similar to another competitor.

Account management issues

Once you have developed and completed an account profile you will need to ensure that you have covered the account management issues properly. This will help you to remain objective and ensure that you are thorough. For example:

- Focus on the potential of the account, not ongoing business only.

- Try to get at least one contact at each of the three levels.

- Look for areas where you can improve the relationship/sales potential.

- Try to influence people in the account to promote your company.

- Be realistic about the account's potential.

- Ensure that purchasing requirements are compatible with your products/services.

- Don't look at technical solutions alone as a way to progress the account.

- Look at account development in a strategic way.

- Be honest about where you are in the sales cycle and what you have/haven't done.

These actions will help you develop the account properly. One of the main benefits of developing an account in this way is that you have a better chance of uncovering sales opportunities. *Once this happens many existing accounts won't feel the need to look at a competitor because they will trust you to deliver the solution and offer value for money!*

Identifying and satisfying an account's buying criteria has two other distinct benefits:

1   If an account's buying criteria change, you will able to see this at an early stage

2   You will have more time to influence the 'key players' and ensure that an application is met by your product/service

You will also need to consider the sales strategy of your competitors. They will try to persuade your target accounts and customers to prioritise on benefits that favour their requirements. If you are aware of what you are up against in an account, you will be better prepared to deal with the situation and overcome it.

Other strategic questions

The type of account you are progressing will determine the amount of information you need to understand. It is useful to ask yourself some other 'strategic' questions about the account and answer them. This will give you and other relevant colleagues/management an opportunity to understand target Accounts' buying motivation.

The types of questions you should ask include:

- What products/services do they sell?

- Are they part of any other company/group? If so, who?

- Who are their main competitors, (if so, are you a supplier to any of them)?

- What is your history in the account?

- What is their performance/growth (over past 5 years)?

- What is the path of their decision-making process?

- What are your distinguishing selling points (D.S.P's) over the competition?

Knowing the answers to these questions can have enormous benefits especially if the account has a structured buying process. *It can help when the amount of the potential sale is large or of high strategic value to you.*

Attention to detail

It will be your attention to detail in the 'sales issues' areas that will help you develop an account well, covered in Chapter 1 – Preparation and sales development, (*Recording sales call information*). These issues remain the focus for most companies. You should ensure that you have asked questions in these areas.

You can also do a SWOT analysis (to assess your strengths, weaknesses, opportunities and threats in the account). This will help you look at your position and decide what action to take

These points will help you to create an advantage in a target account. To achieve this you will have to invest time in getting to know each account's buying motivation and company culture. This will help you assess the account's potential.

Analysing your sales performance

Another way of making the most of your selling skills is analyse your own sales performance. Many companies do this by focusing on two areas:

- your sales performance against an agreed target; and

- the 'Key Performance Indicators' – K.P.I's – that define company objectives.

The more effective you can be in a number of defined areas the more you will sell.

This can help you compare areas that you do well in with ones that need development and coaching. By identifying and getting better in these areas you will find it easier to develop a sale well. It will also help you to focus on opportunities that have more chance of resulting in a sale.

Benchmarking

One way to manage your sales performance is to develop a forecasting model (as defined in Chapter 1 – Preparation and development, (*Forecasting future sales*)).

Another is to create a set of parameters that can help you to 'benchmark' the main parts of the sales process. In order to do this you will need:

- An agreed standard (appointments, presentations, quotes/ proposals etc).

- A sales target value.

- You and your company's 'buy in' to the process.

- To analyse statistics over a period of time (one month, three months).

The reason it is necessary to do this is that a salesperson might be good at opening a call and developing the relationship but he/she might need more development in presenting or negotiating. Separate sales appointments into first, ongoing and closing appointments. Any calls that don't relate directly to developing a sale should be listed separately. This will make it easier to focus on appointments against which your sales performance can be more easily measured.

Before you introduce a performance ratio table, write down the type of ratios you are looking to achieve. For example:

- A first appointment.

- Three 'on-going' appointments.

- A presentation/demonstration.

- A proposal.

- A closing appointment.

Although not all salespeople's ratios will be the same as your template, it will give you a benchmark to work from. Ensure that you set a realistic target that includes the quality of appointments.

By creating a table to look at your appointment-to-sales ratios, you will be able to compare a level of expectation against what was achieved. It will make it easier to see in which areas you are performing well and where development is needed. This will help you avoid wasting time and ensure that you focus on the accounts that are most likely to result in a sale.

The following table looks at an ideal salesperson's performance in a one-month period. It includes a breakdown of the proposed number of first, on-going appointments, proposals, presentations and closing appointments to achieve one order. The results of this can then provide statistical information in the form of a percentage ratio. E.g. in this example, you would expect 33% of proposals to turn into orders.

Benchmarking/Key Performance Indicators

Benchmarking/Key Performance Indicators	Monthly targets
a. Ideal number of actual orders expected (per month) =	a. 5
b. Target value of orders per month = 5 x 10,000 units per order =	b. 50,000 units
c. Ideal number of first appointments (per month) =	c. 20
c. Ideal number of ongoing sales appointments (per month) =	d. 30
e. Ideal number of proposals =	e. 15
f. Ideal number of presentations (per month) =	f. 10
g. Ideal number of closing appointments (per month) =	g. 8

Ideal appointment to order ratio (as a percentage) = 10%. That is c. + d. divided by a.(%)

= For every ten appointment you expect to get one order

Ideal value of each appointment = 1,000 units. That is b. divided by (c. + d.)

= Order value divided by the number of all appointments that month, excluding account management/closing appointments

Ideal proposal to order ratio of = 33%. That is b. divided by e.(%)

= Order value divided by the number of proposals sent this month

Ideal closing appointment to order ratio = 62%. That is a. divided by g.(%)

NB. A letter (e. for example) followed by a percentage sign (%) means that the letter is shown as a percentage total (not number or value)

Benefits of benchmarking for managers

Benefits in being able to analyse this type of information (whether you are a sales person or manager) is that you will be able to:

- Breakdown your sales cycle (and identify areas of strengths and weakness).

- Measure any 'gaps' that exist and address them with training/ coaching.

- Encourage salespeople to take more responsibility for developing a sale well.

An order is made up of a number of defined actions at each stage of the sales cycle. By breaking down these stages and analysing them, you will be in a better position to know how to maintain and improve sales performance.

Statistical information is a useful management tool to help members of a sales team maximise their skills. It should be noted that every salesperson is an individual and will have a different approach to the stages of the sales cycle. For example, take someone who is above target but does not meet your minimum sales performance indicators. If you are a manager, care should be taken to set standards that don't discourage successful salespeople. However, this should not be used as an excuse for poor sales behaviour by someone who exceeds a target.

Benchmarking targets should be fair and realistic. There should be some margin for error and a way of tracking sales performance over a period of time – perhaps three to six months. Other factors that will affect how well it works include someone's ability, experience and general approach to the sales role.

Selling is about getting results, by meeting customer needs, and building business relationships. By monitoring your sales activity, you will have a better understanding of your strengths and weaknesses. Knowing this will also improve your chances of not wasting time and effort in the wrong areas. It will also highlight areas where any sales development is needed in order for you to become more effective.

Chapter summary

In this chapter we have looked at:

- Managing target accounts and relationships.

- Developing an account strategy.

- Analysing your sales performance.

Breaking in to new accounts is a vital part of the sales process, maintaining and developing them is another. In this chapter we have looked at how important it is to manage your accounts well and build good business relationships. This can be done by understanding the target account's market, buying motivation and decision-making process.

You can track information by creating an 'Account Profile', which will help you create a sales strategy. This will improve your chances of selling more of your products/services, by breaking down the actions that are needed to develop an account well.

We have focused on how you can analyse the stages of your own sales cycle and set ideal standards of activity. These can then be compared with your actual results. This will help you understand what areas you need to focus on in order to become more effective.

Key points

- ✓ Building trust in an account is a key part of any customer/supplier relationship.

- ✓ Understand a target account's D.S.P's (Distinguishing Selling Points).

- ✓ Get to know different contacts who influence the sales process.

- ✓ Spend time developing a strategy to win/grow your key accounts.

- ✓ Analyse your performance by benchmarking your sales activity.

Coaching table

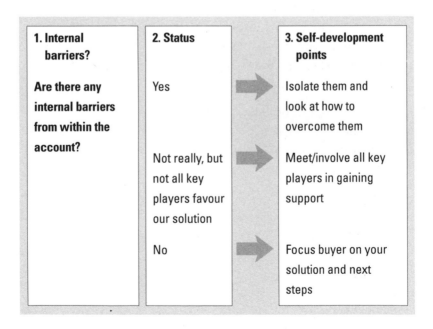

1. Internal barriers?	2. Status	3. Self-development points
Are there any internal barriers from within the account?	Yes	Isolate them and look at how to overcome them
	Not really, but not all key players favour our solution	Meet/involve all key players in gaining support
	No	Focus buyer on your solution and next steps

The 10 do's and don'ts of successful selling

Do	Don't
1 *Get on first name terms* with your target account contacts	*Don't try and 'cut corners'.* This will only result in more objections later in the sale and a focus on price!
2 *Be interested in people* and try to be interesting!	*Don't close too early* for an order; ensure that you have genuine commitment!
3 *Develop one stage of a sale well* before moving to the next	*Don't blame other people,* even if they make a mistake. Look for commitment from them to solve an issue and focus on the solution!
4 *Get to know different types of people* in an account – influencers, the decision-maker and senior managers	*Don't keep blaming yourself* if you make mistakes. Learn from them; try not to repeat them!
5 *Relate your solution to a target account's need* when you present your products/services	*Be honest with yourself* – you will only lose sales if you don't!
6 *Maintain a high level of motivation.* Avoid negative people where possible – or try and get them to focus on the positives!	*Don't talk about your products too early in the sale* – think of ways of gaining commitment first

7 *Look for commitment* at **every** stage of the sales cycle	*Don't expect a competitor's loyal customer to be loyal to you!*
8 *Commit yourself* to being thorough and managing yourself and your time well	*Don't see self-development as a chore,* but as an opportunity to improve your selling skills to help you sell more!
9 *Understand a target account's buying cycle* and level of expectation	*Don't be too busy!* This is a sign that you are not managing yourself well. It can also lead to stress!
10 *Plan the time in your week* to look at how you can develop your target accounts	*Don't rely on buyers to get back to you.* Look to contact them at an agreed date and time.

Thorogood publishing

Thorogood publishes a wide range of books, reports and psychometric tests. Listed below is a selection of key titles.

Desktop Guides

The marketing strategy desktop guide   *Norton Paley* • £16.99

The sales manager's desktop guide
                              Mike Gale and Julian Clay • £16.99

The company director's desktop guide   *David Martin* • £16.99

The credit controller's desktop guide   *Roger Mason* • £16.99

The company secretary's desktop guide   *Roger Mason* • £16.99

The finance and accountancy desktop guide
                                             Ralph Tiffin • £16.99

The commercial engineer's desktop guide   *Tim Boyce* • £16.99

The training manager's desktop guide   *Eddie Davies* • £16.99

The PR practitioner's desktop guide   *Caroline Black* • £16.99

Win new business – the desktop guide   *Susan Croft* • £16.99

Masters in Management

Mastering business planning and strategy   *Paul Elkin* • £14.99

Mastering financial management   *Stephen Brookson* • £14.99

Mastering leadership   *Michael Williams* • £14.99

Mastering negotiations   *Eric Evans* • £14.99

Mastering people management   *Mark Thomas* • £14.99

Mastering personal and interpersonal skills
                                             Peter Haddon • £14.99

Mastering project management   *Cathy Lake* • £14.99

Business Action Pocketbooks

Edited by David Irwin

Building your business pocketbook	£6.99
Developing yourself and your staff pocketbook	£6.99
Finance and profitability pocketbook	£6.99
Managing and employing people pocketbook	£6.99
Sales and marketing pocketbook	£6.99
Managing projects and operations pocketbook	£6.99
Effective business communications pocketbook	£6.99
PR techniques that work	*Edited by Jim Dunn* • £6.99
Adair on leadership	*Edited by Neil Thomas* • £6.99

Other titles

The John Adair handbook of management and leadership
Edited by Neil Thomas • £24.99

The inside track to successful management
Dr Gerald Kushel • £12.99

The pension trustee's handbook (3rd edition)
Robin Ellison • £25

Boost your company's profits
Barrie Pearson • £12.99

Negotiate to succeed
Julie Lewthwaite • £12.99

The management tool kit
Sultan Kermally • £10.99

Working smarter
Graham Roberts-Phelps • £14.99

Test your management skills
Michael Williams • £15.99

The art of headless chicken management
Elly Brewer and Mark Edwards • £6.99

EMU challenge and change – the implications for business
John Atkin • £11.99

Everything you need for an NVQ in management
Julie Lewthwaite • £22.99

Customer relationship management
Graham Roberts-Phelps • £14.99

Time management and personal development
John Adair and Melanie Allen • £10.99

Sales management and organisation   *Peter Green* • £9.99

Telephone tactics   *Graham Roberts-Phelps* • £10.99

Companies don't succeed people do!
Graham Roberts-Phelps • £12.99

Inspiring leadership   *John Adair* • £15.99

The book of ME   *Barrie Pearson and Neil Thomas* • £14.99

The complete guide to debt recovery   *Roger Mason* • £12.99

Janner's complete speechmaker   *Greville Janner* • £10.99

Gurus on business strategy   *Tony Grundy* • £14.99

Dynamic practice development   *Kim Tasso* • £29.99

Thorogood also has an extensive range of reports and special briefings which are written specifically for professionals wanting expert information.

For a full listing of all Thorogood publications, or to order any title, please call Thorogood Customer Services on **020 7749 4748** or fax on **020 7729 6110**. Alternatively please view our website at **www.thorogood.ws**.